Virginia Slave Births Index

1853-1865

Volume 6
Geographic Supplement

Alexandria Library
Special Collections Branch

Leslie Anderson
Editor

Ada Valaitis, Assistant Editor

HERITAGE BOOKS
2014

HERITAGE BOOKS
AN IMPRINT OF HERITAGE BOOKS, INC.

Books, CDs, and more—Worldwide

For our listing of thousands of titles see our website
at
www.HeritageBooks.com

Published 2014 by
HERITAGE BOOKS, INC.
Publishing Division
5810 Ruatan Street
Berwyn Heights, Md. 20740

Heritage Books by the author:

Obituary Notices from the Alexandria *(Virginia)* Gazette, *1784-1915*
Lloyd House, Alexandria Library Staff

Virginia Slave Births Index, 1853-1865,
Alexandria Library, Local History/Special Collections
Volume 1, A-C
Volume 2, D-G
Volume 3, H-L
Volume 4, M-R
Volume 5, S-Z
Volume 6, Geographic Supplement

International Standard Book Numbers
Paperbound: 978-0-7884-5558-2
Clothbound: 978-0-7884-9011-8

INTRODUCTION

In 1853, the Commonwealth of Virginia began an annual registration of births and deaths. The *Birth Index of Slaves, 1853-1865* was later transcribed by the Work Projects Administration (WPA) and recorded on microfilm. While the information—name of informant, infant's name, mother's name, birth date, place of birth—is of immense value to genealogists, working with the microfilm can be problematic. Hence, the creation of this multi-volume reference work, *Virginia Slave Births Index, 1853-1865*.

The microfilm is available at Alexandria Library, Special Collections Branch, in Alexandria, Virginia as "Birth Index of Slaves,1853-1865 (VA)" #00079 and at the Library of Virginia, in Richmond, Virginia as "1A Birth Index: 1853-1866."

Two items in the "Introduction" for the previous volumes deserve attention. The first item refers to "slave owner surname (or corporate owner)." The slave owner *might* have been the informant but someone else, for example, an overseer, a neighbor, or a relative might have reported the birth. The second item refers to "(mu)" which was far more likely an abbreviation for "mulatto" than "multiple births."

It is important to emphasize that the *Virginia Slave Births Index, 1853-1865* points to *birth registers*. Once the researcher has identified an informant, s/he should examine the county or city birth register for additional information. Birth registers for this period are on microfilm at the Library of Virginia.

The *Geographic Supplement* will assist those whose research has led them to a locale rather than to an informant. Counties and cities are alphabetized. There is an alphabetized list of informants for each locale. Regardless of the *number of informants* in a locale who share a surname (or corporate name), or the *number of births* reported by an informant in that locale, the surname (or corporate name) appears only once. There are some instances when the *Virginia Slave Births Index, 1853-1865* reported two locales for one birth. The researcher should examine the birth register of the *first* named county (or city) for additional information.

A review of Record Group 69: Records of the Work Projects Administration (WPA), Series 69.5.5: Records of the Federal Writers' Project (FWP) and Series 69.5.6: Records of the Historical Records Survey (HRS) failed to produce instructions for WPA staff who were involved in the project.

The researcher unfamiliar with Virginia geography should consult historical maps. Each locale, unless otherwise stated, is a county. Some counties are extinct. Certain counties could be mistaken for cities:

> Charles City County
> Elizabeth City County (extinct)
> James City County

Several counties and cities have the same name:

> Alexandria County (extinct) & Alexandria (city)
> Norfolk County (extinct) & Norfolk (city)
> Richmond County & Richmond (city)
> Roanoke County & Roanoke (city)

In 1863, some Virginia counties were lost to the newly formed West Virginia. However, the *Birth Index of Slaves, 1853-1865*, which was transcribed by the WPA, did not include those former Virginia counties.

Any database is only as good as the data entry. While we have made every effort to be accurate, mistakes are unavoidable.

Leslie Anderson, Editor
Reference Librarian
Alexandria Library
Special Collections Branch
717 Queen Street
Alexandria, Virginia 22314-2420

May 2014

Virginia Slave Births Index, 1853-1865, Geographic Supplement

Accomack	Accomack	Accomack
Abdal	Chandler	Evans
Ailworth	Chapman	Ewell
Allen	Coard	Eyre
Ames	Coleburn	Fiddeman
Ashby	Coleman	Field
Aydelott	Colona	Finney
Ayres	Colonel	Fletcher
Badger	Colonna	Floyd
Bagwell	Colony	Folio
Baker	Conquest	Fosque
Bayly	Copes	Garrison
Bayne	Corbin	Gillespie
Bell	Cropper	Glenn
Beloate	Curtis	Godwin
Berry	Custis	Grant
Bird	Davis	Gunter
Boggs	Dickerson	Hack
Booker	Dix	Haisy
Bradford	Doughty	Hale
Brickhouse	Downing	Hall
Brittingham	Drummond	Hannon
Brodwater	Dunton	Hannun
Brown	East	Hargis
Browne	Edmonds	Harmanson
Bull	Edmonis	Harmon
Bunting	Edwards	Harris
Burton	Eichleberger	Heath
Byrd	Elliott	Henderson

Virginia Slave Births Index, 1853-1865, Geographic Supplement

Accomack	Accomack	Accomack
Hersley	Mears	Scarborough
Hickman	Melson	Scarburgh
Hinman	Moore	Scherer
Hoisy	Nock	Shield
Holding	Northam	Slocomb
Holland	Parker	Smith
Hope	Parkes	Snead
Horsey	Parks	Stewart
Hossee	Parramore	Stran
Hutchinson	Pettit	Stratton
Hyslop	Phillips	Straw
Jarvis	Pitts	Stuart
Johnson	Poulson	Sturgis
Jones	Powell	Tankard
Joynes	Read	Taylor
Justice	Revel	Tull
Kellam	Rew	Turlington
Langsdale	Richardson	Turner
Lecato	Right	Tweedy
Lewis	Riley	Twiford
Lilliston	Robbins	Upshur
Littiteston	Roberts	Waddy
Major	Rodgers	Waistcoat
Mapp	Rogers	Walker
Marshall	Ross	Walls
Martin	Rue	Walston
Mason	Russell	Walter
Matheny	Satchele	Walters
Mathews	Satchell	Ward
Matthews	Savage	Warren

Virginia Slave Births Index, 1853-1865, Geographic Supplement

Accomack	Albemarle	Albemarle
Watson	Bayley	Bull
West	Bibb	Bunces
White	Birckhead	Burch
Wilkins	Birkhead	Burk
Willis	Black	Burnders
Wise	Blackwell	Burnham
Wright	Blain	Burnley
Wyatt	Blair	Burrass
Young	Bledsoe	Burruss
Accomack/Northampton	Boaz	Cabell
Powell	Bowcock	Campbell
Waddy	Bowen	Carden
Albemarle	Bowin	Carpenter
Abel	Bows	Carr
Abell	Boxe	Carrington
Alexander	Boyd	Carter
Allen	Boyden	Carver
Ames	Brady	Cary
Anderson	Brag	Catterton
Antrin	Bramham	Chapman
Appling	Branch	Chewning
Austin	Branham	Chick
Baber	Britt	Childress
Bailey	Broadhead	Christian
Ball	Broadus	Clark
Ballard	Brockman	Clarke
Barksdale	Brown	Cleaveland
Barnett	Browne	Clements
Barrett	Browning	Cleveland
Bates	Buckner	Clopton

Virginia Slave Births Index, 1853-1865, Geographic Supplement

Albemarle	Albemarle	Albemarle
Cobbs	Darnielle	Earley
Cochran	Darrow	Early
Cocke	Davis	Eddes
Coleman	Dawson	Edge
Coles	Day	Edwards
Collins	Detter	Elliote
Colster	Dettor	Elliott
Colston	Dickenson	Elsom
Cook	Dickerson	English
Cooke	Diggs	Estes
Cosby	Dinwiddie	Estis
Cowheard	Dollins	Eubank
Cowherd	Dossey	Evans
Cox	Dossie	Everett
Craig	Douglas	Faber
Crank	Douglass	Farish
Craven	Dowell	Farneyhough
Crawford	Drew	Farnezhough
Creel	Driscole	Farrar
Crenshaw	Duke	Farrow
Crobarger	Dulaney	Ferguson
Crockran	Duncan	Ferneyhough
Crowbarger	Dunkin	Fife
Crump	Dunkum	Finks
Dabney	Dunn	Fitch
Dameron	Durett	Fitz
Damoron	Durrett	Fitzhugh
Damron	Dyjes	Flannagan
Daniel	Eades	Forbes
Darnelle	Eads	Foster

Virginia Slave Births Index, 1853-1865, Geographic Supplement

Albemarle	Albemarle	Albemarle
Fray	Goss	Higginbotham
Fretwell	Gougham	Hill
Fry	Graham	Hogan
Furguson	Graves	Holcombe
Gambell	Grayham	Holladay
Gant	Grayson	Holloday
Gantt	Griffin	Hornsey
Garett	Hall	Howard
Garland	Hamlet	Huckstep
Garrett	Hamlett	Hudson
Garth	Hamner	Hughes
Gay	Hancock	Hurt
Gentry	Hansborough	Jackson
Geonine	Hansborro	Jarman
George	Hansbrough	Jarmon
Giannini	Harden	Jefferies
Gibbs	Hardin	Jefferson
Gibson	Harlan	Jeffreys
Gilbert	Harlow	Jeffries
Gilliam	Harper	Johnson
Gillum	Harris	Johnston
Gilmen	Harrison	Jones
Gilson	Hart	Jury
Glover	Hartman	Keblinger
Gooch	Hartsock	Keister
Goodloe	Hartsook	Kelly
Goodman	Haskins	Keyton
Goodwin	Head	Kidd
Goolsby	Herd	Lacey
Gordon	Herndon	Lannahan

Virginia Slave Births Index, 1853-1865, Geographic Supplement

Albemarle	Albemarle	Albemarle
Leathers	May	Moss
Leitch	Mayne	Munday
Lennahan	Mayo	Mundy
Levy	Mayor	Musgrove
Lewis	McCleod	Nailer
Lindsay	McClunn	Naylor
Lively	McGehee	Nelson
Livily	McGhee	Newman
Lobban	McIntire	Nicholas
Locker	McKenney	Noland
Lofland	McKennie	Norris
Lowell	McKinnie	Norval
Lowery	McLeod	Norvell
Lowry	McSparren	Oaks
Lyones	McVeigh	Oldham
Macon	Mead	Oliver
Maddox	Meade	Omohundro
Madison	MeGehee	Owen
Magruder	Merewether	Owens
Maher	Meriweather	Pace
Mann	Merriwether	Page
Mannoni	Michie	Parish
Marshall	Mills	Parrish
Martin	Minor	Parrot
Mason	Moon	Parrott
Massey	Moore	Patrick
Massie	Moran	Patterson
Mathews	Morris	Patton
Maupin	Morrison	Payne
Maury	Mosby	Pegram

Albemarle	**Albemarle**	**Albemarle**
Pendleton	Robinson	Sigfree
Perkins	Rodes	Sigourney
Perrow	Rogers	Simmes
Peyton	Ross	Simms
Phillips	Rothwell	Simpco
Poindexter	Rozer	Sims
Pollard	Ruffin	Sinclair
Poore	Sadler	Slack
Porterfield	Salmon	Smith
Powell	Sampson	Snead
Preedy	Sandidge	Snead & Chewning
Prentis	Sandridge	Sneed
Prentiss	Saunders	Southall
Price	Scott	Sowell
Railey	Scribner	Spicer
Ramsay	Scruggs	Spiece
Ramsey	Segfreed	Spooner
Randolph	Seigfrid	Sprouse
Ransay	Seigfried	Stachlin
Razor	Shackelford	Staples
Rea	Shackleford	Starke
Reives	Shacklin	Staton
Reynolds	Shafer	Stephens
Rhodes	Sharpe	Stephenson
Richards	Shelton	Stevens
Riley	Shepherd	Stevenson
Rittenhome	Shiflett	Stockton
Rittenhouse	Shotwell	Stout
Rives	Shultz	Strachlin
Roberts	Sigfred	Strange

Virginia Slave Births Index, 1853-1865, Geographic Supplement

Albemarle	Albemarle	Albemarle
Suddarth	Topkins	Wiatt
Sullivan	Townley	Wilhoit
Sutherland	Townly	Wilkerson
Sutton	Travillian	Williams
Taylor	Trevillian	Wilson
Teal	Trice	Wingfield
Tebbs	Tucker	Winston
Teel	Tunstal	Wolfe
Terrell	Tunstall	Wood
Terrill	Tupton	Woods
Thacker	Turner	Woodson
Therman	Twyman	Wooldridge
Thomas	VanDoren	Wright
Thompkins	Via	Wyant
Thompson	Wade	Wyatt
Thomson	Walker	Yager
Thornley	Wallace	Yancey
Thurman	Walter	Yates
Thurmond	Walters	**Alexandria**
Thurston	Walton	Clark
Tilman	Ward	**Alexandria Co**
Tilmon	Watson	Adam
Timberlake	Wayland	Addison
Tinsley	Wayt	Alexander
Tomason	Wells	Allison
Tomkins	Wertenbaker	Andrews
Tompkins	West	Arnold
Toney	Wheeler	Ashby
Tool	White	Baggott
Toole	Wiant	Ball

Virginia Slave Births Index, 1853-1865, Geographic Supplement

Alexandria Co	Alexandria Co	Alexandria Co
Bayne	Hart	Sulivan
Beach	Hicks	Summers
Berkley	Hollinsbury	Swann
Brent	Hunter	Thomas
Brockett	Huntson	Thompson
Brodus	Irwin	Watts
Burch	Johnston	Welsh
Campbell	Jordon	Wheat
Cassanove	Keens	**Alleghany**
Cazenover	Kincheloe	Allen
Crier	King	Boswell
Custis	Lacey	Brown
Douglass	Lee	Burk
Emmerson	Mason	Clark
English	Masters	Crow
Evans	Minor	Damron
Febry	Monroe	Douglas
Frazier	Partlow	Eakin
Gardon	Perry	Ervine
Garrell	Roberson	Fudge
Gordan	Robinson	Gilliland
Gorden	Sangster	Griffith
Gordon	Scarce	Hansbarger
Gregg	Scott	Hook
Guinn	Shacklett	Jackson
Guy	Slaughter	Jordan
Hall	Smith	Jordon
Harden	Smoot	Karnes
Harper	Sommers	Kyle
Harris	Stephenson	Layne

Virginia Slave Births Index, 1853-1865, Geographic Supplement

Alleghany	Amelia	Amelia
Lively	Baldwin	Brown
Mallon	Banister	Burk
Mallow	Barden	Burke
Mann	Bardin	Burton
Massie	Barksdale	Cadwell
McKenny	Barsdale	Carsley
McKinney	Barton	Carter
McMahon	Bass	Chaffin
Morton	Baugh	Chaffins
Payne	Berkeley	Chapman
Persinger	Blair	Chappell
Pitzer	Bland	Chappen
Rucker	Blanton	Cheatham
Shirkey	Boisseau	Childress
Sively	Bolling	Christian
Steele	Bonus	Clare
Thermond	Booker	Clark
Tinsley	Booth	Clarke
Walker	Boothe	Clary
Williams	Borden	Clay
Woodward	Bordin	Clayton
Alleghany/Botetourt	Bott	Clore
Johnson	Bottom	Cocke
Amelia	Botts	Cole
Adams	Bowman	Coleman
Allen	Bowry	Colley
Anderson	Bragg	Coraley
Angel	Branch	Corsley
Archer	Brazeal	Cosby
Bailey	Bridgeforth	Cottrell

Virginia Slave Births Index, 1853-1865, Geographic Supplement

Amelia	Amelia	Amelia
Cousins	Flowkes	Holcombe
Craddock	Foster	Holt
Cralley	Fowlkes	Howlett
Crally	Fowlks	Hubbard
Crenshaw	Fretwell	Hurt
Crowder	Gee	Jackson
Davis	Gills	Jefferson
Dearen	Glenn	Jenkins
Dearran	Goode	Jeter
Deaton	Graves	Johns
Delaney	Green	Johnson
Dunavent	Gregory	Jones
Dunn	Grigg	Kidd
Dunnavant	Hall	Knight
Dunnavent	Hamblan	Land
Dyson	Hamblin	Lane
Eanes	Hamlin	Layne
Easley	Hardaway	Letellier
Echols	Harris	Littlepage
Eckols	Harrison	Lockett
Eggleston	Harvie	Loving
Ellington	Haskew	Lund
Ellis	Haskins	Maben
Evans	Hastings	Major
Farley	Hawkes	Mann
Farmer	Hawks	Marshall
Farrar	Hendrick	Mason
Fassar	Hillman	Masters
Featherston	Hillsman	Matthew
Fitzgerald	Hobson	Matthews

Virginia Slave Births Index, 1853-1865, Geographic Supplement

Amelia	Amelia	Amelia
Maxey	Old	Steger
Mayo	Oliver	Stringer
McCune	O'Sullivan	Tabb
McGehee	Palmore	Taliaferro
McGoods	Perkinson	Talliaferro
Mead	Peyton	Tallieferro
Meade	Phillips	Taylor
Meader	Pleasants	Thomas
Meador	Pollard	Thompson
Meaux	Pride	Tinsley
MeGehee	Quarles	Townes
Merryman	Ranson	Towns
Miles	Rives	Traylor
Mileston	Roberts	Tucker
Miller	Robertson	Turner
Millston	Robinson	Vandensen
Moore	Rowlett	Vandenson
Morgan	Rowlette	Vandnesen
Morris	Rutherford	Vandneson
Morriss	Sadler	Vaughan
Motley	Saint Clair	Waddell
Mottley	SaintClair	Wade
Musgrove	Sanderson	Wallace
Neal	Schmucker	Walthall
Neatharey	Scott	Ware
Neathery	Seay	Warrinar
NeGehee	Smith	Warriner
Noble	Smithey	Warring
Norfleet	Southall	Wathall
Nunnally	St. Clair	Webster

Virginia Slave Births Index, 1853-1865, Geographic Supplement

Amelia	Amherst	Amherst
Wells	Barnes	Coffee
White	Barret	Coghill
Whitworth	Barrett	Coleman
Wiley	Baughson	Conley
Wilkenson	Bennett	Cox
Wilkerson	Bethel	Cunningham
Wilkinson	Bethell	Curle
Williams	Blair	Dameron
Williamson	Brag	Davenport
Wills	Bray	Davies
Willson	Broaddus	Davis
Wilson	Brockman	Dawson
Wily	Brown	Day
Wingo	Burford	Dearing
Wood	Burks	Dillard
Woodrum	Burley	Dilliard
Wooldridge	Cabell	Dox
Woolridge	Camden	Drummond
Worshall	Camm	Dudley
Worsham	Campbell	Duncan
Wright	Carson	Edwards
Amherst	Carter	Ellet
Allen	Cash	Ellis
Ambler	Cheatwood	Eubank
Ammonett	Chewning	Farrer
Amonett	Childress	Fletcher
Anderson	Childs	Flood
Appling	Christian	Fogus
Bailey	Claiborne	Franklin
Barley	Clark	Gannaway

Virginia Slave Births Index, 1853-1865, Geographic Supplement

Amherst	**Amherst**	**Amherst**
Garland	Irvine	Mason
Gilbert	Jeffries	Massie
Gooch	Jennings	Mathew
Goode	Johns	Mathews
Goodwin	Johnson	Matthew
Grimm	Joiner	Mays
Hargrove	Jones	McAlexander
Harris	Jordain	McChany
Harrison	Jordan	McDaniel
Heirkle	Keith	McDonald
Heiskell	Kent	McIver
Henley	Kidd	Mecher
Henly	Knight	Meeker
Henry	Knights	Mer-?
Henson	Kyle	Miles
Hicks	Lamkin	Miller
Higgenbotham	Landrum	Milliner
Higginbotham	Layne	Millner
Hill	Lee	Mitchell
Hite	Leftwich	Moriss
Hix	Logan	Morris
Hollingsworth	Long	Morriss
Hollinsworth	Love	Mosby
Hopkins	Loving	Mosely
Howl	Lovy	Mosley
Hudson	Magruder	Mountcastle
Hurley	Mahone	Mundy
Hutcherson	Mantiply	Neblett
Hutcheson	Marion	Noel
Hylton	Martin	North

Virginia Slave Births Index, 1853-1865, Geographic Supplement

Amherst	Amherst	Amherst
Ogden	Richeson	Swan
Old	Ridgeway	Swann
Omohondro	Robertson	Taliaferro
Omohundro	Robeson	Taylor
Page	Robinson	Terry
Pain	Rose	Thomas
Paris	Royster	Thompson
Parks	Rucker	Thornton
Parr	Ruth	Tinsley
Patteson	Rutherford	Toler
Paxton	Sandidge	Tucker
Pendleton	Saundige	Tucker & Henley
Penn	Scott	Turner
Pervis	Settle	Tyree
Peticola	Shackleford	Wade
Pettit	Shelton	Walker
Pettitt	Shepherd	Waller
Pettyjohn	Sheppard	Ware
Phillips	Shrader	Warrick
Pierce	Simpson	Warwick
Pleasants	Smith	Watson
Poindexter	Snead	Watts
Powell	Spencer	Waugh
Proffit	Spiller	Weiler
Pryor	Splueer	Wheeler
Quarles	Stanfield	White
Ramsey	Staples	Whitehead
Reynolds	Steen	Williams
Rhoads	Stephens	Wills
Richerson	Story	Wilson

Virginia Slave Births Index, 1853-1865, Geographic Supplement

Amherst	Appomattox	Appomattox
Wingfield	Brightwell	Dickinson
Winn	Brown	Dillard
Winston	Burford	Dinguid
Wood	Burks	Diuguid
Woodroof	Caldwell	Doss
Woods	Calhoun	Dunnington
Wright	Canon	Durphey
Appomattox	Carson	Elam
Abbitt	Carter	Elliott
Abbott	Carwiles	Evans
Adams	Cawthon	Farrar
Agee	Cawthorn	Fears
Alvis	Cawthorne	Fetcher
Anderson	Cheadle	Fitch
Arington	Cheatham	Fitcher
Arrington	Christian	Fleshman
Atkinson	Clark	Flippin
Atwood	Clarke	Flood
Bagby	Coleman	Forbes
Baker	Conner	Ford
Barnard	Corson	Fore
Bascoville	Cousins	Foster
Baskerville	Crews	Franklin
Bass	Daniel	Furbush
Beckham	Davidson	Gannaway
Biglow	Davis	Garland
Binford	Day	Garrett
Bobock	Dearman	Gary
Bocock	Dearmon	Gillespie
Branch	Dickerson	Gilliam

Virginia Slave Births Index, 1853-1865, Geographic Supplement

Appomattox	Appomattox	Appomattox
Gills	Johns	Owens
Glenn	Johnson	Palmer
Glover	Jones	Pamplin
Goff	Kelley	Pankey
Gough	Kyle	Paris
Goush	LeGrand	Patterson
Gray	Lewis	Patteson
Gunter	Mann	Paulett
Hamner	Marshall	Pelly
Hancock	Martin	Penn
Hannah	Mathews	Perkins
Harden	Matthews	Petty
Hardy	McDaniel	Phelps
Harris	McDearmon	Pinnell
Harvey	McIver	Pittman
Hile	McKinney	Plunkett
Hill	McNamee	Porter
Hills	Miller	Portwood
Hix	Mills	Quisenberry
Hood	Mitchell	Reveley
Howerton	Moore	Revely
Hughes	Morgan	Richardson
Hunter	Morris	Rively
Hurt	Moseley	Robertson
Inge	Moss	Roush
Isbell	Mundy	Roushe
Jenkins	Neighbors	Routen
Jennings	North	Rush
Jinkins	Nowlin	Scruggs
Jinnings	Overton	Sears

Virginia Slave Births Index, 1853-1865, Geographic Supplement

Appomattox	Appomattox	Augusta
Shearer	Whealer	Anderson
Simmons	Wheeler	Antrin
Smith	White	Argenbright
Snapp	Whitehead	Ashmucker
Snell	Williams	Bare
Staples	Wilson	Barger
Stewart	Wingfield	Bashaw
Stickley	Woodall	Bashew
Stickly	Woode	Baylor
Stone	Woodson	Bear
Stratton	Wooldridge	Beard
Swan	Wright	Bell
Tanner	Wyatt	Bennet
Taylor	**Appomattox/Amherst**	Berry
Thomas	McKinney	Black
Thompson	**Appomattox/Buckingham**	Blackwood
Thornhill	Branch	Bourland
Thornton	Harris	Bradley
Tibbs	Johnson	Brawford
Tidball	**Appomattox/Campbell**	Bridge
Trent	Marshall	Brooks
Tuggle	**Appomattox/Charlotte**	Brown
Turner	Garland	Brownlee
Vawter	**Augusta**	Bruce
Walker	Abney	Bryan
Walton	Achord	Buchanan
Watkins	Acord	Bumgardner
Watson	Alexander	Burwell
Webb	Allen	Bush
West	Ande	Calbreath

Virginia Slave Births Index, 1853-1865, Geographic Supplement

Augusta	Augusta	Augusta
Caldwell	Dalhouse	Fuller
Calhoun	Davidson	Fulton
Camron	Davis	Gamble
Cannon	Demasters	Gambles
Carson	Dice	Gardner
Chapman	Doake	Garner
Christ	Doke	Gay
Christian	Dold	Gibbs
Churchman	Dudley	Gilkerson
Clark	Dunlap	Gilkeson
Clayton	Dunlop	Gillum
Claytor	Eadson	Gipson
Clemmar	Edison	Givens
Cline	Eidson	Glendy
Coalter	Ellis	Glover
Cobbs	Emmerson	Gooch
Cochran	Ervin	Graham
Coiner	Ervine	Gray
Collins	Ewing	Greiner
Cooper	Faber	Gross
Corson	Fauber	Grove
Coyhill	Finley	Guthria
Coyner	Fishburn	Guthrie
Crabb	Fitch	Guy
Craig	Foner	Hailman
Craun	Forrer	Hall
Crawford	Fox	Hamilton
Crist	Frazier	Hanger
Crobarger	Freeman	Harden
Cullen	Fretwell	Harman

Virginia Slave Births Index, 1853-1865, Geographic Supplement

Augusta	Augusta	Augusta
Harmon	Keller	Massie
Harner	Kennedy	Maupin
Harnsbarger	Kennerly	McChesney
Harper	Kenney	McClanahan
Harris	Kerr	McClanham
Hart	Killion	McClung
Hawpe	King	McClure
Hendren	Kinney	McComb
Hendron	Kiser	McCormick
Henebarger	Koiner	McCue
Henry	Lambert	McCure
Hernsberger	Lange	McCutchan
Herring	Laren	McCutchen
Hill	Lease	McGuffin
Hite	Leneave	McNutt
Hitt	Leneve	McPheeters
Hobb	Lepley	McPheters
Hodge	Lesley	Merrett
Hogshead	Lessley	Merritt
Hopkins	Lewis	Messersmith
Howell	Lightner	Miller
Hudson	Lipscomb	Mills
Humphrey	Loffland	Mish
Humpreys	Long	Mitchell
Hunter	Lowman	Moffett
Irvin	Lynn	Moffitt
Irvine	Mackey	Montgomery
Johnson	Mann	Moore
Johnston	Marshall	Moorman
Keiser	Martin	Morris

Augusta	Augusta	Augusta
Moseley	Sellers	Trice
Nelson	Shaw	Trimble
Netherland	Sheffey	Umphrey
Opie	Sheilds	VanLear
Orebaugh	Shields	Via
Ott	Shirey	Vigar
Padgett	Shuey	Waddell
Parkins	Shumate	Waddle
Patrick	Simms	Walker
Patterson	Smith	Wallace
Pelter	Speck	Washington
Peyton	Spotts	Watson
Philips	Sproul	Wayland
Phillips	Sprowl	Webb
Pilson	Steele	Whitecomb
Pitman	Steigle	Whitmon
Poage	Sterrett	Whitmore
Randolph	Stockart	Willson
Reed	Stoddard	Wilson
Reeves	Stout	Wonderlick
Richardson	Strouse	Wood
Rivercomb	Stuart	Wren
Robertson	Stump	Wright
Rogers	Summerson	Young
Ruff	Swartzell	**Bath**
Rush	Swisher	Bell
Sale	Swoope	Bolar
Samuels	Tate	Bollar
Schumaker	Thompson	Bonner
Scott	Todd	Bratton

Virginia Slave Births Index, 1853-1865, Geographic Supplement

Bath	Bath	Bath/Augusta
Bryan	Mann	Glendy
Burke	Mastoe	**Bedford**
Burns	Mayse	Acre
Cameron	McChesney	Adams
Campbell	McClentic	Agnew
Cauley	McClintic	Allen
Cavendish	McClung	Anderson
Cawley	McDannald	Andrew
Clark	McDannold	Andrews
Cleek	McElwes	Anthony
Coberly	McGuffin	Arington
Dangerfield	Morrison	Armistead
Ervin	Mustoe	Armstead
Francisca	Payne	Arrington
Francisco	Porter	Arthur
Frazier	Randolph	Ashwell
Gatewood	Shields	Austin
Given	Shumate	Barker
Glendy	Simmons	Bayer
Goode	Sithington	Bedford
Grim	Sively	Bell
Gwin	Strother	Bellamy
Hickman	Terrill	Bilbro
Hopkins	Thomas	Board
Johnson	Warwick	Boling
Johnston	Weaver	Bond
Kincaid	Williams	Bowles
Lockridge	Wilson	Brown
Lyle	Wise	Buckner
Madison		Buford

Virginia Slave Births Index, 1853-1865, Geographic Supplement

Bedford	Bedford	Bedford
Burford	Cobbs	Early
Burks	Cobler	Elliott
Burnett	Cochran	English
Burroughs	Cofer	Eubank
Burwell	Coffer	Everett
Cabb	Coleman	Everitt
Callaway	Comer	Ewing
Calloway	Compton	Falls
Caloway	Crawford	Fariss
Campbell	Creasey	Farris
Camper	Creasy	Farriss
Canefix	Crenshaw	Ferguson
Carnefix	Cruggs	Ferrel
Carner	Crump	Ferrell
Carnifax	Cundiff	Ferril
Carnifix	Dameron	Fields
Carter	Damron	Finsley
Chalmers	Davis	Fitzpatrick
Chappell	Dawson	Fizer
Cheatum	Dearing	Forger
Cheatwood	Dent	Forgie
Chewning	Dewitt	Fowler
Chilton	Dickenson	Frailing
Christian	Dickerson	Fraling
Clay	Dickinson	Franklin
Clayter	Dobyns	Fuqua
Clayton	Donald	Garnett
Claytor	Douglass	Garrett
Clemons	Dowell	Gibbs
Cobb	Dunton	Gill

Virginia Slave Births Index, 1853-1865, Geographic Supplement

Bedford	**Bedford**	**Bedford**
Gills	Hicks	Kent
Goad	Higginton	Knight
Goard	Hobson	Lacker
Goggin	Hoffman	Lancaster
Good	Holt	Lane
Goode	Hopkins	Lange
Goodman	Hubbard	Layne
Graves	Huddleston	Lazenby
Gray	Hudnall	Lee
Grigsby	Hughes	Leftwich
Gwatkin	Hunt	Leyburn
Gwatkins	Hunter	Lockie
Halley	Hurt	Logwood
Hally	Hutter	Loury
Halsey	Irvine	Lowry
Hancock	Izard	Loyd
Hanes	Jacobs	Luck
Hardy	James	Lumpkin
Harris	Jennings	Lynch
Harrison	Jeter	Major
Harriss	Johnson	Mansfield
Hart	Jones	Markham
Hatcher	Joplin	Marsh
Hatter	Jopling	Marshall
Hawkins	Jordan	Martin
Headen	Jordon	Matthews
Heck	Karey	Mayo
Heptenstall	Kasey	Mays
Heptinstall	Kelso	McCabe
Hewitt	Kelsow	McClain

Bedford	**Bedford**	**Bedford**
McClintock	Mumford	Phelps
McDaniel	Musgrove	Poage
McGhee	Myler	Poindexter
McLain	Mylor	Pollard
McManaway	Nance	Powell
McMullen	Nelms	Preas
Mead	Nelson	Preston
Meador	Newsom	Prince
Meadow	Newsome	Pullen
Mennis	Nichols	Purcell
Meriweather	Noel	Quales
Merriman	Noell	Quarles
Merriweather	Nowell	Radford
Merriwether	Ogden	Read
Merryman	Oglesby	Redue
Metcalf	Ore	Redus
Metcalfe	Otey	Reese
Miler	Overstreet	Reynolds
Miller	Pagett	Rice
Millner	Paggitt	Roberts
Minnis	Parker	Robertson
Minter	Parrow	Robinson
Mitchell	Pate	Rosebrough
Moorman	Patterson	Rosebrugh
Morgan	Payne	Ross
Morris	Pearce	Roy
Mosby	Penn	Royalty
Moseley	Perkins	Rucker
Mosely	Perrow	Ruker
Moulton	Peters	Rusher

Virginia Slave Births Index, 1853-1865, Geographic Supplement

Bedford	Bedford	Bedford
Rusko	Terry	Wiggington
Sale	Thaxton	Wigginton
Sales	Thomas	Wight
Saunders	Thomason	Wigington
Schenk	Thomasson	Wilkerson
Scott	Thompson	Wilks
Scruggs	Thomson	Williams
Shaon	Thurman	Williamson
Sharp	Thurmon	Wilson
Shelton	Tinsley	Wingfield
Siner	Tompkins	Winston
Skinnell	Trent	Witt
Slaughter	Turner	Wood
Sledd	Turpin	Woolfolk
Smelser	Updike	Worley
Smith	Wade	Wright
Speece	Walker	**Bedford/Botetourt**
Spinner	Walkes	Haller
Spradling	Watson	**Bland**
Spruce	Watts	Allen
Stephens	Wells	Bishop
Steptoe	West	Brown
Stiff	Wheat	Crockett
Stone	Wheeler	Crump
Stratton	White	Davidson
Sublett	Whitely	Grayson
Swain	Whitlow	Hoge
Talbot	Whitten	Morton
Tanner	Whorley	Newberry
Taylor	Wiggenton	Robinett

Bland	Botetourt	Botetourt
Smith	Caldwell	Gibson
Walthal	Camper	Gilbert
Wesendonek	Carper	Gilliam
Botetourt	Carrington	Gillian
Allen	Cartmell	Gilmore
Alphin	Casper	Gorges
Ammen	Circle	Grant
Ammon	Coffman	Grasty
Ammons	Coiner	Gray
Anderson	Cook	Guggenheimer
Baker	Copeland	Haden
Banks	Copland	Hailman
Beale	Cornelius	Hamman
Bell	Couch	Hammon
Biggs	Curd	Hannah
Bishop	Davis	Harvey
Blair	Deigher	Haydon
Bonsack	Dickey	Henkle
Booze	Dill	Hobson
Bower	Dobson	Hoilman
Bowyer	Eugart	Holeson
Boyd	Farrow	Holston
Breckenridge	Ferrell	Hudson
Breckinridge	Ferrill	Huff
Brownlee	Firebaugh	Jeter
Brugh	Flaherty	Johns
Burk	Fluke	Johnson
Burkholder	Garland	Johnston
Burks	Gault	Kean
Burwell	Gibbs	Kelly

Botetourt	Botetourt	Botetourt
Kerns	Noffsinger	Shaver
Kitly	Nofsinger	Shickel
Kyle	Noftsinger	Shields
Lackland	Obenchain	Shirkey
Lacks	Obenshain	Snider
Lancaster	Owens	Snodgrass
Langhorn	Parks	Spiller
Langhorne	Patton	Stevens
Lee	Payton	Stoner
Leib	Peary	Stull
Lemmon	Peck	Switzer
Lemon	Peery	Thomas
Lockett	Pelagrew	Thompson
Luck	Pendleton	Thrasher
Maelick	Penn	Trevy
Markham	Pettigrew	Turpin
Martin	Phillips	Utz
Maupin	Pitzer	Valentine
Mayo	Price	Vineyard
Mays	Radford	Vinyard
McCluer	Reid	Waggoner
McClure	Reynolds	Wagoner
McDowell	Richardson	Walkup
McFallan	Roberson	Walrond
McFallon	Robinson	Watkins
McFerran	Rowland	Watson
Miller	Sails	Williams
Morton	Sales	Williamson
Nace	Samuels	Wilson
Neville	Saville	Womack

Virginia Slave Births Index, 1853-1865, Geographic Supplement

Botetourt	Brunswick	Brunswick
Wood	Blunt	Clark
Woodson	Bolling	Clarke
Botetourt/Roanoke	Bonner	Clary
Stevens	Bowden	Clayton
Brunswick	Bowen	Cleaton
Aberbnathy	Bradley	Cock
Allen	Bradly	Cocke
Anderton	Branch	Coleman
Archer	Branscomb	Connelly
Astrop	Braswell	Cordis
Atkins	Brewer	Crichton
Bailey	Briggs	Crowder
Baird	Britt	Crutchfield
Barner	Broadnax	Cunningham
Barron	Brodnax	Dameron
Barrow	Broune	Daniel
Bass	Browder	Davie
Batte	Brown	Davis
Baugh	Buford	Delbridge
Beckwith	Burge	Dix
Bennett	Cabiness	Doyle
Biggs	Callis	Dromgoole
Birdsong	Carpenter	Drummond
Birthright	Carroll	Duane
Bishop	Cary	Duggar
Blackwell	Castleman	Dugger
Blanch	Chambliss	Dunn
Bland	Cheely	Eanes
Blanks	Christopher	Edmonds
Blick	Claiborne	Edmonis

Virginia Slave Births Index, 1853-1865, Geographic Supplement

Brunswick	Brunswick	Brunswick
Edmund	Hall	Johnson
Edmunds	Hamilton	Jolley
Edwards	Hamlett	Jolly
Ellis	Hamlin	Jones
Elmore	Hammock	Judd
Eppes	Hardy	Justice
Epps	Harison	Kelly
Erzell	Harper	Kennedy
Evans	Harris	Kidd
Ezell	Harrison	King
Feild	Harriss	Kirk
Ferguson	Hartwell	Kirkland
Field	Harwell	Lambert
Finch	Haskins	Lashley
Flinn	Hawkins	Lett
Flourney	Hawthorn	Lewis
Flournoy	Hawthorne	Littleton
Ford	Heartwell	Love
Fraser	Hicks	Lucy
Freeman	Hines	Lundy
Gibbon	Hite	Lynch
Gill	House	Maclin
Gilliam	Howell	Maddox
Goodrich	Howerton	Maddux
Gray	Huckstep	Mallory
Green	Huff	Malone
Gregg	Huskey	Mangum
Griffin	Husky	Mangus
Griggs	Ingram	Manley
Hagood	Jennings	Manning

Virginia Slave Births Index, 1853-1865, Geographic Supplement

Brunswick	Brunswick	Brunswick
Manson	Peebles	Saunders
Mason	Percival	Scoggin
Mathews	Percivall	Scoggins
Matthews	Perkins	Seward
Meacham	Perkinson	Seymour
Meade	Phillips	Sharp
Meredith	Phipps	Sharpe
Merritt	Pitchford	Shell
Montgomery	Pope	Short
Moore	Porch	Sills
Morgan	Powell	Sims
Morris	Power	Slate
Morrison	Poyner	Smith
Mosely	Poynor	Speaks
Moss	Price	Spenser
Nanny	Pritchett	Stainback
Neblett	Proctor	Stanley
Nicholson	Puryear	Stanly
Noble	Rainey	Steed
Northington	Raney	Steward
Ogburn	Rawlings	Stith
Orgain	Rice	Stone
Owen	Riddick	Stors
Palmer	Rives	Strange
Parham	Robinson	Stuart
Patillo	Rogers	Sturdivant
Pattells	Rose	Tally
Pattillo	Ross	Taylor
Peace	Samford	Temple
Pearson	Sanford	Thacker

Brunswick	Brunswick	Brunswick/NC
Thomas	Wilkes	Lucy
Thompson	Wilkins	**Brunswick/Sussex**
Thrower	Williams	Kirby
Tighman	Williamson	**Buchanan**
Tillman	Winfield	Mullins
Tilman	Winfree	**Buckingham**
Towler	Winn	Abraham
Travis	Worsham	Adams
Traylor	Wray	Agee
Trotter	Wright	Allen
Tucker	Wyatt	Alvis
Tudor	Wyche	Anderson
Turnbull	Wynn	Apperson
Vaiden	**Brunswick/Albemarle**	Appling
Vaughan	Douglas	Austin
Vick	**Brunswick/Amelia**	Ayers
Wade	Rives	Ayres
Walker	**Brunswick/Dinwiddie**	Baber
Wallace	Moore	Bagby
Waller	**Brunswick/GA**	Bailey
Wallton	Battle	Baily
Walthon	Bishop	Baird
Walton	**Brunswick/Greensville**	Baldwin
Warrick	Blick	Ballow
Warwick	Field	Baughan
Weaver	King	Beard
Webb	Pearson	Berryman
Wesson	**Brunswick/Lunenburg**	Blackwell
Wheeler	Maddox	Blankenship
White		Boatwright

Virginia Slave Births Index, 1853-1865, Geographic Supplement

Buckingham	Buckingham	Buckingham
Bocock	Coleman	Gannaway
Bolling	Cosby	Gantt
Bondurant	Cox	Ganway
Booker	Crute	Garnett
Bowles	Damron	Garrett
Bowman	Darneille	Garrette
Bradley	Davidson	Gary
Branch	Davis	Gauldin
Bransford	Druen	Gaunt
Brooks	Druin	Gibson
Brown	Duncan	Gillespie
Bryant	Dunkum	Gilliam
Bumpass	Dunn	Gillian
Bumpus	Dunnavant	Gillispie
Burruss	Dysart	Gills
Cabell	Elcan	Glover
Call	Eldridge	Gooch
Carden	Ellis	Goolsby
Carter	Epperson	Gordon
Cason	Eppes	Gough
Chambers	Evans	Goughenouer
Chapell	Farrow	Gregg
Chappell	Ferguson	Gregory
Chastaine	Fitzgerald	Grigg
Christian	Flood	Guerrant
Claiborne	Fones	Guthrey
Clarke	Fontaine	Guthrie
Clay	Forbes	Hall
Cobbs	Ford	Hamner
Cocke	Fuqua	Hardiman

Buckingham	Buckingham	Buckingham
Hardwick	Justis	Montague
Hariman	Kidd	Moon
Harris	Kinney	Moore
Harvey	Kyle	Morgan
Haskins	Lackland	Morris
Haynes	Lancaster	Morrisett
Hesse	Layne	Morton
Hickok	Leake	Moseley
Hill	Lee	Moss
Hocker	Leitch	Murphy
Holbrook	Lewis	Nagland
Holman	Mason	Neighbors
Hooper	Maxey	Neighbours
Horseley	Mayo	Newton
Horsley	McConnell	Nicholas
Howell	McCormick	Nixon
Hubard	McCraw	Noel
Hubbard	McDeamon	Norvell
Huddleston	McGehee	Nowell
Hudgin	McKinney	Nuchols
Hudgins	McKinnie	Nuckols
Hudnall	Meador	Nunaly
Huge	Meadow	Nunnally
Hughes	Meredith	Oliver
Irving	Miller	Page
Jackson	Mills	Pankey
Jefferson	Mitchell	Panky
Johns	Molley	Parrack
Johnson	Molloy	Patterson
Jones	Molloyd	Patteson

Buckingham	Buckingham	Buckingham
Perkins	Seargent	Tindall
Pettus	Seay	Toney
Phelps	Sergeant	Trent
Philips	Sharp	Tucker
Phillips	Sharpe	Turner
Pittman	Shaw	Twyman
Pollard	Shepard	Tyler
Powell	Shepherd	Vaughan
Pratt	Simmons	Walker
Price	Sipe	Walton
Putney	Slough	Watson
Pyatt	Smith	West
Ragland	Smyth	White
Randolph	Snead	Whitehead
Ranson	Snoddy	Whitworth
Rees	Spencer	Wilkerson
Reese	Spenser	Wilkins
Reynolds	Stegar	Wilkinson
Riddle	Steger	Williams
Roberts	Stewart	Wilson
Robertson	Stinson	Wise
Robinson	Stratton	Womack
Routon	Stuart	Wood
Rowton	Swoope	Woodall
Sanders	Tapscott	Woodfin
Sargeant	Taylor	Woods
Saunders	Tent	Woodson
Scott	Thomas	Wooldridge
Scrugg	Thompson	Woolridge
Scruggs	Thornton	Word

Virginia Slave Births Index, 1853-1865, Geographic Supplement

Buckingham	Campbell	Campbell
Worsham	Babcock	Carwiles
Wright	Bailey	Cary
Yarbrough	Baily	Cawthon
Zekiel	Barber	Cawthorn
Buckingham/Albemarle	Barksdale	Chambers
Glover	Barrett	Charlton
Harris	Bass	Christian
Buckingham/Appomattox	Bateman	Clark
Bocock	Betterton	Clarke
Buckingham/Cumberland	Blankenship	Clay
Trent	Booker	Clement
Buckingham/Nelson	Booth	Cobbs
Roberts	Bradley	Cock
Buckingham/Petersburg	Brady	Cocke
Gregory	Bramlett	Cohns
Campbell	Briggs	Connelley
Abbitt	Brooks	Connelly
Abbott	Brown	Cook
Adams	Bruce	Cough
Alexander	Burroughs	Cowling
Anderson	Burton	Cox
Andrews	Callaway	Craddock
Anthony	Callehan	Crawford
Apperson	Calloway	Creasy
Armistead	Campbell	Cunningham
Arnold	Candler	Curle
Arrington	Carden	Dabney
Arthur	Cardwell	Daniel
Asher	Carter	Daniels
Ashlin	Carwile	Day

Campbell	Campbell	Campbell
Dean	Epps	Glass
Deane	Estes	Glenn
Dearing	Estus	Goodman
Depriest	Evans	Gough
Deprist	Ewart	Graham
Dew	Faris	Haden
Dews	Fariss	Hake
Dillard	Farmer	Hall
Dinwiddie	Farris	Halsey
Diuguid	Farriss	Hamersly
Dixon	Finch	Hamlet
Doss	Fitch	Hamner
Douglas	Flagg	Hancock
Douglass	Flemmings	Hart
Driskell	Fleshman	Harvey
Drury	Flood	Hawkins
Duke	Floyd	Hayth
Earley	Flynn	Hazlewood
Early	Fore	Henderson
East	Foster	Hendrick
Echols	Fox	Henry
Edley	Franklin	Herndon
Edmunds	Frazier	Hewitt
Edwards	Frazure	Hicks
Elam	Gardner	Hillsman
Elliot	Garland	Hobson
Elliott	Gilchrist	Hollins
Emanuel	Gill	Holt
Emmerson	Gilliam	Homer
Epperson	Gills	Horner

Virginia Slave Births Index, 1853-1865, Geographic Supplement

Campbell	Campbell	Campbell
Horton	Lee	Moore
Howard	Leeson	Moorman
Hoytt	LeGrand	Morgan
Hubbard	Lemmon	Moseley
Hudnall	Lindsay	Mundy
Hughes	Lipscomb	Munroe
Hunter	Litchford	Murrell
Hurst	Luson	Murrill
Hurt	Lynch	North
Hutter	Maddox	Nowlin
Irvin	Mallory	Oglesby
Irvine	Marshall	Organ
Ivey	Martin	Owen
Jackson	Mason	Owens
Jefferson	Mathews	Padget
Jennings	Matthews	Padgett
Johnson	Mattox	Page
Jones	Mays	Pannill
Jordan	McCorkle	Patrick
Kabler	McCraw	Payne
Kean	McDaniel	Perkins
Keene	McIver	Perrow
Kinnear	Merrill	Pettigrew
Knight	Merritt	Phelps
Lambeth	Michie	Phillips
Land	Miles	Poindexter
Langhorne	Miller	Poole
Lawson	Mohr	Poore
Lazenby	Monroe	Porter
Leason	Moon	Price

Virginia Slave Births Index, 1853-1865, Geographic Supplement

Campbell	Campbell	Campbell
Pryor	Steptoe	Walton
Pucket	Stevens	Ward
Puckett	Stewart	Warwick
Reid	Stone	Washington
Reveley	Swinney	Weaver
Reynolds	Tanner	Whitlow
Rice	Tardy	Whitton
Richardson	Taylor	Wiatt
Roach	Tease	Wightman
Robertson	Teass	Wilkerson
Robinson	Templin	Willbourn
Roper	Templine	Williams
Rosser	Terrell	Wilmouth
Rucker	Terry	Wilson
Russell	Thornhill	Wimbish
Ryan	Thurman	Wimbish & Co
Saunders	Torrence	Winfree
Scott	Trent	Wingfield
Shands	Tucker	Winston
Shepperson	Tweedy	Winter
Simpson	Twiford	Withers
Smith	Tynes	Wood
Smith & Gibson	Unna	Wooding
Snow	Upton	Woodroof
Speece	Urquehart	Woodson
Spence	Urquhart	Wooling
Spencer	Vaughan	Woolling
Spuce	Wade	Wright
Staples	Walker	Wyatt
Staten	Walthall	Wylie

Virginia Slave Births Index, 1853-1865, Geographic Supplement

Campbell	Caroline	Caroline
Wyllie	Baylor	Butler
Young	Beazley	Butter
Younger	Bell	Callawn
Yuille	Bentley	Campbell
Campbell (B in Buckingham)	Berkley	Care
Christian	Bernard	Carnal
Campbell/Appomattox	Berry	Carneal
Elliott	Bibb	Carrick
Campbell/Halifax	Bibbs	Carter
Young	Blades	Cash
Caroline	Blanton	Catlate
Acres	Blaydes	Catlett
Allen	Boulware	Chandler
Alsop	Boutwell	Chapman
Ancarrow	Bowers	Chennult
Anderson	Bowie	Chewning
Andrew	Broaddus	Chiles
Andrews	Broaddy	Clark
Armstrong	Brooks	Clarke
Atkinson	Bruce	Clarkis
Bagby	Buckner	Coalter
Baker	Bullock	Coates
Ball	Burgher	Coats
Barbee	Burk	Cobb
Barris	Burke	Cobbs
Bataile	Burkeley	Cogbill
Bataille	Burkley	Coghill
Bates	Burnard	Coiner
Battaile	Burrus	Cole
Battaill	Burruss	Coleman

Virginia Slave Births Index, 1853-1865, Geographic Supplement

Caroline	Caroline	Caroline
Collins	Ellis	Hargrave
Conduit	Eubank	Hargrove
Conner	Farish	Harris
Conway	Farrish	Harrison
Corbin	Fitzhugh	Henderson
Corbins	Flippi	Henly
Corbit	Flippo	Henshaw
Coultery	Fortune	Hill
Cox	Fox	Hockett
Crump	Friend	Holloway
DeJarnatte	Garnett	Houston
DeJarnett	Garrett	Hudgins
DeJarnette	Gatewood	Hundley
Denney	George	Hunter
Dew	Gibbs	Hurt
Dick	Glassell	Hutcheson
Dickenson	Goodloe	James
Dickins	Goodwin	Jarrell
Dickinson	Gorden	Jerrald
Diggs	Gordon	Jerrell
Dillard	Goulden	Jerrold
Doggett	Gouldin	Jesse
Donahoe	Gouldman	Jessee
Downing	Gravatt	Jeter
Dunn	Gray	Johnson
Durrett	Green	Johnston
Durvin	Greenstreet	Jones
Duval	Guest	Jordan
Duvall	Hackett	Jordon
Dyson	Hancock	Kane

Virginia Slave Births Index, 1853-1865, Geographic Supplement

Caroline	Caroline	Caroline
Kay	Mashall	Pare
Kean	Mason	Parker
Keane	Massie	Parr
Keezee	Maury	Partlow
Kelley	McCallay	Peatross
Kelly	McCalley	Pendleton
Kemp	McCally	Penney
Kidd	McKenney	Penny
Lafoe	McKey	Peyton
Langdon	McLaughlin	Phillips
Lefoe	McLoclin	Pittman
Lewis	McSpindle	Pitts
Lightfoot	Meredith	Pollard
Long	Merryman	Powers
Longan	Micon	Pratt
Longebelin	Micow	Pruett
Loughlin	Miller	Puller
Loven	Mills	Quarles
Lucas	Minter	Quesenberry
Luck	Moncure	Ramsey
Lumpkin	Moor	Ramsy
Lumpkins	Morris	Redd
Lunsford	Motley	Reives
Madison	Munday	Rennolds
Mahon	Newton	Reynolds
Mahone	Noel	Richards
Mallory	Nore	Richardson
Malone	Norment	Richerson
Marshall	Oliver	Richeson
Martin	Page	Riddle

Virginia Slave Births Index, 1853-1865, Geographic Supplement

Caroline	Caroline	Caroline
Rixey	Sutton	Upshaw
Roan	Swann	Urquhart
Roane	Taliaferro	Walker
Roberson	Taylor	Waller
Robinson	Temple	Ware
Rollins	Tennent	Washington
Roper	Terrell	Weagleworth
Rosser	Terrill	Welch
Rowe	Terry	West
Royston	Thomas	White
Sale	Thornby	Wigglesworth
Samuel	Thorne	Williamson
Samuell	Thornley	Wiltshire
Samuels	Thornton	Winn
Saunders	Tod	Winston
Schooler	Todd	Withers
Scott	Tompkins	Wood
Seay	Toombs	Woodfork
Shaddock	Travillan	Woolfolk
Shadduck	Travillian	Woolfork
Shepherd	Trevilian	Wortham
Sirls	Trevillian	Worthem
Skinker	Tribble	Wright
Smith	Trible	Wyatt
Smoot	Trice	Yates
Southworth	Tuck	Young
Spindle	Tuning	**Caroline/Amelia**
Sterne	Tunstall	Dunn
Stevens	Turner	**Caroline/Madison, KY**
Streshley	Tyler	Welch

Carroll	Charles City	Charles City
Bobbitt	Baylor	Holdcroft
Boyd	Binns	Hopkins
Carter	Bowry	Hubbard
Crawford	Bradley	Jerdon
Davidson	Bright	Jerdone
Davison	Brown	Johnson
Earley	Butler	Jones
Early	Carter	Jordon
Elliott	Christian	Jordone
Ferguson	Clarke	Keesee
Furgurson	Clay	Kelser
Gardner	Clopton	Ladd
Jennings	Crenshaw	Lamb
Kinzer	Douthat	Lawrence
Kirkbride	Eppes	Lipscomb
Kyle	Ferguson	Maddox
McFarland	Fergusson	Major
Potter	Folkes	Marable
Vaughan	Gary	Marston
Vinson	Gay	McKinney
Watson	Gentry	McManus
Charles City	Gill	Minson
Adams	Goddin	Morecock
Alexander	Graves	Moss
Apperson	Gregory	Mountcastle
Armistead	Harrison	Nance
Armstead	Harwood	New
Baker	Haxall	Orgain
Ball	Hayes	Otey
Barnes	Haynes	Parker

Charles City	Charles City	Charlotte
Pearman	Weymack	Berkeley
Peirce	Willcox	Berkley
Pemberton	Wills	Berry
Phillips	Willson	Booker
Pierce	Wilson	Booth
Pollard	Young	Boothe
Roach	**Charlotte**	Boswell
Roane	Adams	Boulden
Rock	Agela	Bouldin
Rowland	Alexander	Breedlove
Royall	Allen	Brightwell
Ruffin	Almond	Britton
Selden	Anderson	Broocks
Smith	Andrews	Brooks
Southall	Angles	Brown
Stagg	Armistead	Bruce
Starke	Armstead	Bugg
Stubblefield	Arvin	Buster
Talman	Atkins	Callaham
Taylor	Bacon	Campbell
Towney	Bailey	Cardwell
Townley	Baines	Carrington
Turner	Baker	Carter
Tyler	Baldwin	Cary
Upshaw	Barbee	Chaffin
Vaiden	Barksdale	Chandler
Waddill	Barnes	Chappell
Wade	Barter	Clark
Walker	Bedford	Clarke
Ware	Bell	Clary

Virginia Slave Births Index, 1853-1865, Geographic Supplement

Charlotte	Charlotte	Charlotte
Clements	Driskill	Fuqua
Cock	Duffer	Furgurson
Cole	Duke	Gaines
Collins	Duncan	Gains
Comfort	Dunnington	Garden
Compton	Dupree	Garland
Conner	Edmonds	Garner
Cook	Edmonis	Garnett
Cox	Edmund	Garrett
Crafton	Edmunds	Gaulden
Crawford	Edwards	Gauldin
Crawley	Eggleston	Gaulding
Crawly	Elam	Gillespie
Crews	Elliott	Gilliam
Crump	Elliotte	Gillispie
Crutcher	Estes	Glenn
Crute	Eudailey	Goode
Curtis	Featherson	Gordon
Custis	Featherston	Gouldin
Daniel	Ferrel	Goulding
Davenport	Ferrell	Green
Davidson	Flournoy	Grigsby
Davis	Ford	Guthery
Dennis	Fore	Guthrey
Deshazer	Foster	Guthrie
Devenport	Fowler	Haily
Dickenson	Fowlkes	Hamersley
Dickerson	Freeman	Hamilton
Dickinson	Friend	Hamlet
Driskell	Fugua	Hamlett

Virginia Slave Births Index, 1853-1865, Geographic Supplement

Charlotte	Charlotte	Charlotte
Hancock	Jennings	McGhee
Hankins	Johns	McNinney
Hannah	Johnson	McNinnie
Harden	Johnston	McNinny
Hardiman	Jones	McPhail
Hardy	Kirkpatrick	Melone
Harris	Laine	Michie
Hart	Lawson	Middleton
Harvey	Layne	Mills
Harvy	Ledbetter	Moffitt
Haskins	Lee	Mohorn
Hatcher	LeGrand	Moon
Hatchett	Lewis	Morehorn
Henry	Ligon	Morgan
Hill	Lipscomb	Morrison
Hilton	Lipscombe	Morton
Hinds	London	Moseley
Hines	Lyle	Mosely
Hobson	Mack	Moses
Hodge	Maddison	Nath
Holt	Madison	Nelson
Howell	Malone	Nichols
Hundley	Maloney	North
Hunter	Marshall	Osborn
Hutcherson	Martin	Osborne
Hutcheson	Mason	Osburne
Hutchinson	Mastin	Overby
Jackson	Mathews	Owen
Jefferson	McCargo	Palmer
Jeffress	McGehee	Paris

Virginia Slave Births Index, 1853-1865, Geographic Supplement

Charlotte	Charlotte	Charlotte
Paulett	Robertson	Tucker
Peele	Robinson	Turnbull
Peete	Rose	Vaughan
Pegg	Rosser	Vawter
Pentecost	Schmidt	Venable
Perkinson	Scott	Waddill
Persell	Shepperson	Wallace
Pettus	Shorter	Walton
Pollard	Sims	Watkins
Price	Skidmore	Watson
Priddy	Slaughter	Wayt
Proctor	Smith	Webb
Pryor	Snell	White
Pugh	Southall	Whitehead
Purcell	Spencer	Whitworth
Puryear	Spraggins	Wilbon
Raine	Spragins	Wilkes
Ralls	Stephenson	Wilkins
Ramsay	Stewart	Willbourn
Ramsey	Tally	Williams
Ranson	Tatum	Williamson
Rawlins	Taylor	Wilson
Read	Thomas	Wood
Redd	Thompson	Woods
Redmon	Thornton	**Charlotte/Appomattox**
Redmond	Tombs	Snell
Rice	Toombs	**Charlotte/Buckingham**
Richardson	Toons	Thornton
Roach	Townes	**Charlotte/Campbell**
Roberts	Trent	Driskell

Virginia Slave Births Index, 1853-1865, Geographic Supplement

Charlotte/Campbell
Smith
Trent

Charlotte/Giles
Collins
Morton

Charlotte/Hanover
Duke

Charlotte/Lunenburg
Arvin
Nelson
Williams

Charlotte/Mecklenburg
Hodge
Jeffress

Charlotte/Prince Edward
Robertson

Chesterfield
Adams
Adkins
Allen
Ammonnett
Amonette
Archer
Ashbrook
Atkerson
Atkinson
Bacon
Bailey
Baker
Bass

Chesterfield
Baugh
Beasley
Belcher
Berry
Bishop
Blankenship
Blankinship
Boisseau
Bowles
Bradley
Bragg
Branch
Brander
Bransford
Brewer
Britton
Brooks
Brown
Bruce
Brummall
Bryne
Buffla
Burchet
Burfoot
Burgess
Burnett
Burton
Calvin
Campbell
Chalkley

Chesterfield
Cheatham
Childs
Chiles
Claiborne
Clarke
Clay
Clayton
Cogbill
Cole
Coleman
Colley
Cook
Corling
Cosby
Cotton
Cousins
Covington
Cox
Craddock
Crostick
Crowder
Cundiff
Cunliffe
Curry
Davis
Drakes
Drewry
Duke
Dunn
Dunn & McCrone

Virginia Slave Births Index, 1853-1865, Geographic Supplement

Chesterfield	Chesterfield	Chesterfield
Dunnavant	Fuqua	Hudson
Dunston	Furcron	Ivey
Duval	Gary	Jackson
Dyson	Gates	James
Eanes	Gibbs	Jenks
Eddings	Gifford	Jeter
Edson	Gill	Jewett
Edwards	Gilliam	Johnson
Elam	Godsey	Jones
Ellett	Goode	Jordan
Elliott	Graves	Keach
Ellis	Gregory	Keech
Elliss	Gresham	Keesee
Epps	Groves	Kelley
Farmer	Hall	Kelly
Fendley	Hancock	Kesee
Fendly	Harris	Kinsey
Ferguson	Haskins	Lacy
Fergusson	Hatcher	Lavieng
Fisher	Heath	Leath
Flournoy	Hendrick	Leonard
Ford	Hill	Lipscomb
Fore	Hobbs	Lithgow
Forloine	Hobson	Little
Forsee	Horner	Lockett
Foster	Hoskins	Lundie
Fowlkes	Howard	Lundy
Franklin	Howle	Lynch
French	Howlett	Maddra
Friend	Howlette	Madra

Virginia Slave Births Index, 1853-1865, Geographic Supplement

Chesterfield	Chesterfield	Chesterfield
Manchester	Parrish	Rowlett
Manders	Patram	Royall
Mann	Patteson	Rudd
Markham	Peers	Rudy
Marks	Perdue	Ruffin
Martin	Perkins	Saddler
Marx	Perkinson	Sadler
Mason	Phaup	Salle
McCann	Phillips	Sallie
McGee	Pierce	Scammell
McLaurin	Pinchbeck	Seamarks
McLaurine	Pitchford	Seamonreed
McTyre	Poindexter	Seaward
Michie	Pollard	Seawibryd
Miller	Porter	Sheppard
Montague	Powell	Simason
Montecue	Price	Simonson
Moody	Pulliam	Sims
Moore	Puryear	Sizer
Morrissett	Radford	Smith
Moss	Radliff	Snellings
Murry	Rae	Spears
Newby	Randolph	Strachan
Newell	Ray	Stratton
Nunnally	Reams	Sturdivant
Osborne	Redford	Tatum
Overby	Roberts	Taylor
Overton	Robertson	Temple
Owens	Robinson	Terrill
Page	Roper	Thweatt

Virginia Slave Births Index, 1853-1865, Geographic Supplement

Chesterfield	Chesterfield	Clarke
Thweatte	Woodfin	Cattlett
Tinsley	Wooldridge	Chunn
Tizzard	Worsham	Clark
Tompkins	Young	Clarke
Totty	**Chesterfield/Petersburg**	Clopton
Townes	Olivar	Colston
Trabell	**Clarke**	Cooke
Tucker	Alexander	Copenhaver
Turpin	Allen	Corben
Vaden	Ashby	Corbin
Varnier	Barnett	Crebo
Venable	Bell	Crow
Walke	Berlin	Dearmont
Walker	Berry	Duke
Ward	Blakemore	Earle
Ware	Bonham	Elliott
Watkins	Bowen	Enders
Webster	Bradford	Everhart
Weisiger	Briggs	Fahrner
Wells	Bromley	Fauntleroy
Whitehead	Brown	Feeher
Whitehurst	Bryarly	Foster
Whitlock	Burchell	Frazier
Wilkinson	Burnett	Funsten
Wilson	Burwell	Funston
Winfell	Byerly	Gant
Winfree	Byrd	Glass
Winston	Carter	Gold
Womack	Castleman	Gorden
Wood	Catlett	Grantham

Clarke	Clarke	Clarke
Green	Loutman	Royston
Grigsby	Luke	Rusel
Gruber	Marshall	Russell
Hall	Massey	Rust
Hancocke	McCormick	Shepherd
Hardesty	McGuire	Shively
Harris	McMurray	Shumate
Harrison	McPierce	Skinker
Hay	Meade	Smith
Hefleblower	Mitchell	Smith & Gibson
Hesser	Moore	Sowers
Hite	Morgan	Steele
Howard	Neill	Stribbling
Huyett	Nelson	Stribling
Jackson	Nunn	Strother
Janney	O'Rear	Suter
Johnson	O'Rick	Swan
Jones	Osborn	Swann
Jordan	Page	Tanquary
Jorden	Parkins	Taylor
Kennerly	Pendleton	Thompson
Kerfoot	Pierce	Timberlake
Kimball	Pugh	Trenary
Kindler	Pulliam	Tucker
Kneller	Randolph	Tuley
Knight	Reily	Tuly
Kownslar	Richardson	Vasse
Larue	Richardson & Pent	Walker
Lewis	Riely	Ware
Littleton	Romine	Weir

Virginia Slave Births Index, 1853-1865, Geographic Supplement

Clarke	Craig	Culpeper
Welch	Mills	Bailey
Wheat	Niday	Baine
Whiting	Nutter	Ball
Williams	Peck	Barbour
Craig	Reynolds	Barton
Bishop	Ripley	Bataille
Caldwell	Sarver	Baughn
Carper	Spessard	Beasley
Crist	Stebar	Beckham
Dawson	Thomas	Bell
Dodd	Trenor	Bickers
Donohoe	Trinor	Botts
Eakin	Wagener	Bowen
Farrar	Walker	Bradford
Farrier	Warker	Brannon
Givens	Waugh	Bridges
Givins	Wiley	Bridget
Gray	Younger	Britton
Hannah	**Culpeper**	Broadus
Hawkins	Acker	Brown
Hill	Adams	Browning
Huffman	Alcocke	Bruce
Hypes	Alexander	Buress
Jamison	Allen	Burgess
Jemison	Anderson	Burnley
Jemmerson	Apperson	Burns
Leffel	Appeson	Burton
McCartney	Armstrong	Butler
McPherson	Ashby	Butten
Miller	Ashly	Button

Culpeper	Culpeper	Culpeper
Bywaters	Eggborn	Harris
Carson	Fant	Hawkins
Carter	Fare	Hernden
Chewning	Farish	Herndon
Child	Ficklin	Higgerson
Colbert	Field	Hill
Cole	Finney	Hitt
Coleman	Finny	Hoffman
Colvin	Fitzhugh	House
Conner	Flint	Howison
Conners	Foster	Hudson
Cook	Freeman	Huffman
Cooke	Gaines	Hufman
Coons	Garnett	Hume
Cooper	Gee	Humphrey
Corbin	George	Humphreys
Covington	Gibson	Humpreys
Crigler	Glassell	Hurt
Crittendon	Gordon	Hutcherson
Crump	Gray	James
Cunningham	Grayson	Jameson
Curtis	Green	Jamison
Daniel	Griffin	Jeffries
Day	Grimsley	Jennings
Dayman	Grinnan	Jeter
Doyle	Guinn	Jett
Duncan	Haffman	Jetts
Duncanson	Hall	Jones
Dunkerson	Hamilton	Keith
Eggbon	Hansbrough	Kelly

Virginia Slave Births Index, 1853-1865, Geographic Supplement

Culpeper	Culpeper	Culpeper
Kemper	Nalle	Rudacill
Lake	Neall	Rudasill
Latham	Nelson	Scott
Laurance	Newby	Sedwich
Laurence	Newman	Sedwick
Lewis	Norman	Settle
Lightfoot	Norris	Shackelford
Lillard	O'Bannon	Shadrack
Long	Parr	Shepherd
Luckett	Patten	Shotwell
Luthill	Payne	Slaughter
Luttrell	Pemberton	Smith
Madison	Pendleton	Smoot
Major	Perry	Somerville
Marshall	Petty	Spilman
Martin	Pinkard	Stallard
Mason	Pulliam	Stark
Massey	Rawles	Stone
Matthews	Read	Stout
Mauzy	Redd	Stringfellow
McDermot	Richards	Strother
McDonald	Rixey	Suite
Millan	Roberts	Taliaferro
Miller	Robertson	Tancill
Mitchell	Robson	Tate
Moffett	Rodgers	Taylor
Moncure	Rollings	Thom
Morehead	Ross	Thomas
Morton	Rosser	Thompson
Nall	Royston	Timberlake

Virginia Slave Births Index, 1853-1865, Geographic Supplement

Culpeper	Culpeper/Albemarle	Cumberland
Tinsley	Lewis	Boatright
Tobin	**Culpeper/Fauquier**	Boatwright
Towles	Jennings	Bolling
Triplett	Jones	Booker
Tritt	**Culpeper/Rappahannock**	Bosher
Tutt	Ball	Boston
Utz	**Cumberland**	Bradley
Vaughan	Abraham	Bradshaw
Wager	Abrahams	Bransford
Wale	Adam	Branton
Walker	Adams	Brightwell
Wallace	Agee	Brown
Wallach	Alderson	Bryant
Wallis	Allen	Budd
Wallop	Ames	Caldwell
Wayman	Amonett	Carrington
Welford	Amos	Carter
Wellford	Anderson	Clarke
Wharton	Apperson	Clary
Wheatley	Archer	Clay
Wheatly	Armistead	Clift
Williams	Armstead	Clopton
Willis	Austin	Cocke
Withers	Bagby	Coleman
Wood	Banks	Colman
Yager	Barker	Colwell
Yancey	Baughan	Coupland
Yancy	Berryman	Crowder
Young	Blake	Cushing
	Blanton	Daniel

Virginia Slave Births Index, 1853-1865, Geographic Supplement

Cumberland	Cumberland	Cumberland
Davis	Garrette	Hughs
Dawson	Gibson	Irving
Dean	Gilliam	Isbell
Denham	Gilson	Jackson
Diggs	Glenn	Jeffries
Ding	Glover	Jenkins
Dowdy	Godsey	Johns
Druin	Goodman	Johnson
Dunford	Griffith	Jones
Dunkum	Guthrey	King
Dupee	Guthrie	Leach
Dupey	Gwathmey	Lee
Dupuy	Hall	Lewis
Durham	Harmon	Lipford
Eggleston	Harris	Lipscomb
England	Harrison	Lynn
Farmer	Hatcher	Madison
Flaggin	Hazelgrove	Magehee
Flannagan	Hazlegrove	Mallon
Fleming	Henderson	Martin
Flippen	Hendrich	Maston
Flippin	Hendrick	Matthews
Ford	Hobson	Mayo
Foster	Holeman	McGehee
Frayser	Holman	McLaurine
Fuqua	Hubbard	Meador
Garnet	Huddleston	Merryman
Garnett	Hudgens	Miles
Garnette	Hudgins	Miller
Garrett	Hughes	Minn

Virginia Slave Births Index, 1853-1865, Geographic Supplement

Cumberland	Cumberland	Cumberland
Minor	Rhodes	Trent
Minter	Robertson	Vaughan
Mont	Robinson	Wade
Morrow	Ryals	Walden
Morrows	Sanderson	Walker
Morton	Scott	Walton
Nash	Seay	Watkins
Nelson	Shields	Weymouth
Newton	Sims	Wheeler
North	Smith	Whitlock
Oliver	Southall	Wilkerson
Overton	Spears	Wilkinson
Page	Spencer	Wilson
Palmer	Starkey	Winfree
Palmore	Steger	Wood
Parish	Stiger	Woodfin
Parker	Stone	Woodruff
Parrish	Strange	Woodson
Perkins	Stratton	Wren
Pettis	Swan	Wrenn
Pettus	Swann	Wright
Phillip	Talley	**Cumberland (B in Campbe**
Phillips	Tally	Clay
Philpotts	Tatum	**Cumberland/Amelia**
Powell	Taylor	Palmore
Powers	Thaxton	Wilson
Price	Thornton	**Cumberland/Buckingham**
Raine	Toler	Anderson
Ransone	Towles	Garnett
Reynolds	Tredway	Garrett

Virginia Slave Births Index, 1853-1865, Geographic Supplement

Cumberland/Buckingham	Danville	Dinwiddie
Page	Law	Algood
Cumberland/Powhatan	Lipscombe	Allen
Booker	Lucas	Allgood
Danville	Lyles	Anderson
Atkinson	Millner	Archer
Ayers	Neal	Atkins
Ayres	Pace	Atkinson
Berryman	Price	Bagby
Bethell	Sampson	Bailer
Brown	Slaughter	Bailey
Buford	Smith	Bailor
Burford	Spraggins	Baily
Claibourne	Stokes	Baldwin
Cosby	Sutherllin	Barker
Crews	Terry	Barner
Davis	Watkins	Barnes
Edmonds	Watt	Barrett
Flippen	Williams	Barrow
Giles	Withers	Baskerville
Grasty	Womack	Bass
Gravly	Wooding	Baylor
Green	Wooton	Beasley
Grigg	Wyllie	Bevill
Hobson	**Danville/Bedford**	Bishop
Holcombe	Pace	Bland
Holland	**Dinwiddie**	Blick
Johnson	Aberbnathy	Boisseau
Johnston	Adams	Bolling
Jones	Adkinson	Booth
Kirkpatrick	Alfriend	Bosseau

Virginia Slave Births Index, 1853-1865, Geographic Supplement

Dinwiddie	Dinwiddie	Dinwiddie
Bott	Crittenden	Foster
Bourdon	Crow	Fraser
Branch	Crowder	Frasier
Brander	Crump	Frayser
Branton	Cutler	Frazier
Bristow	Dabney	Friend
Brooks	Dance	Furgerson
Browder	Darby	Garrett
Brown	Davis	Gibbs
Brownley	Dean	Gill
Butler	DeVlaming	Gilliam
Butterworth	Dodd	Goodwyn
Cabaniss	Dodson	Graham
Carr	Douglas	Grammer
Carter	Doyle	Green
Caudle	Drinkwater	Greenway
Chafin	Duval	Gregory
Chandler	Dyson	Gresham
Chappell	Edmonds	Griffin
Cheatham	Edmonis	Grigg
Clark	Edmunds	Griswold
Clarke	Edwards	Gunn
Clay	Emmins	Hall
Clements	Emmons	Hamblin
Coleman	Epes	Hamlin
Cornwell	Feild	Hardaway
Cousins	Ferguson	Hardy
Cowles	Field	Hargrave
Cox	Fisher	Harper
Crawford	Ford	Harris

Virginia Slave Births Index, 1853-1865, Geographic Supplement

Dinwiddie	Dinwiddie	Dinwiddie
Harrison	Martin	Pollard
Hartwell	Mason	Pool
Harwell	McEnery	Powell
Hawkins	McIlwaine	Prentice
Hawks	Meade	Prosize
Heath	Meredith	Rainey
Hill	Mitchell	Raney
Hitchcock	Moody	Rawlings
Hobbs	Moore	Read
Hubbard	Morris	Reade
Jackson	Morton	Reames
Johnson	Moss	Reams
Jolly	Neaves	Reese
Jones	Neives	Richardson
Kidd	Neves	Rives
King	Niblett	Robertson
Kirby	Northington	Robinson
Kirkland	Nottington	Rogers
Kirks	Nunnally	Roney
Lambert	Oliver	Roper
Lanier	Orgain	Rose
Lawrence	Osborne	Royall
Ledbetter	Peebles	Ruffin
Lee	Pegram	Sallard
Lewis	Pennington	Scott
Lucy	Perkins	Shelly
Lunsford	Perkinson	Shore
Major	Pettus	Short
Malone	Pinchback	Smith
Manley	Pinchbeck	Spain

Dinwiddie	Dinwiddie	Dinwiddie/Nottoway
Spicely	West	Pollard
Spiers	Wheeler	**Dinwiddie/Petersburg**
Steel	White	Bonner
Stell	Whitmore	**Dinwiddie/Sussex**
Stine	Whitworth	Mason
Stith	Wilkerson	**Elizabeth City**
Stone	Williams	Adams
Strachan	Williamson	Armistead
Sturdevant	Wills	Bains
Sturdivant	Wilson	Barnes
Sutherland	Winfield	Bates
Sydnor	Worsham	Blakeley
Thacker	Wyatt	Booker
Thomas	Wynn	Brittingham
Thompson	Young	Burke
Thrift	**Dinwiddie/Amelia**	Causey
Thweatt	Archer	Clopton
Torborne	Coleman	Collier
Tucker	**Dinwiddie/Brunswick**	Cooper
Turnbull	Douglass	Core
Turner	**Dinwiddie/King & Queen**	Coulling
Vaden	Duval	Cullenny
Vaughan	**Dinwiddie/Lunenburg**	Darden
Venable	Lambert	Davis
Wainwright	**Dinwiddie/Nottoway**	Decormis
Walker	Bass	Dennis
Watkins	Brown	Dewbre
Watts	Coleman	Downey
Webb	Johnson	Drummond
Wells	Montague	Edwards

Virginia Slave Births Index, 1853-1865, Geographic Supplement

Elizabeth City	Elizabeth City	Elizabeth City
Elliot	Miller	Watts
Elliott	Moore	West
Fletcher	Outten	Westwood
Fraser	Parish	Whitfield
Garrett	Parker	Whiting
Garrow	Parrish	Williams
Giddings	Patrick	Willis
Goodall	Phillips	Wilson
Ham	Powell	Winder
Hendersen	Presson	Wood
Hickman	Robinson	Wray
Hope	Savage	**Elizabeth City/Hampton**
Howard	Schmelz	Booker
Hudgins	Sclater	Brown
Ivy	Segar	Elliott
Jennings	Semple	Garrett
Johnson	Shield	Giddings
Jones	Sinclair	Ham
Joynes	Smith	Howard
Kelly	Stone	Jones
King	Tabb	King
Latimer	Taylor	Massenburg
Lee	Thomas	McIntosh
Lewelling	Thompson	Parker
Lilliston	Topping	Patrick
Lowry	Turnbull	Roach
Mallory	Twiford	Robinson
Marrow	Twine	Roche
Massenburg	Vaughan	Rudd
Mears	Watson	Savage

Virginia Slave Births Index, 1853-1865, Geographic Supplement

Elizabeth City/Hampton	Essex	Essex
Sheild	Boughton	Durham
Wood	Branham	Dyke
Wray	Bray	Ellis
Elizabeth City/York	Broaddus	Faulconer
Moreland	Brockenbough	Fauntleroy
Sinclair	Brockenbrough	Fisher
Wheeler	Broocks	Fogg
Essex	Brooke	Frank
Ainsley	Brooks	Gardner
Ainslie	Brown	Garnett
Andrews	Burk	Gatewood
Armstrong	Burke	Gordon
Atkens	Burnett	Gouldman
Atkenson	Cauthorn	Graves
Atkins	Clarke	Gray
Atkinson	Clarkson	Greenstreet
Baird	Coates	Haile
Banks	Coghill	Harper
Baylor	Coleman	Hart
Beazley	Covington	Haskins
Bentley	Cox	Hawes
Bently	Crow	Henley
Beverley	Croxton	Hill
Beverly	Dearing	Hipkins
Billips	Dillard	Hoskins
Bird	Dishman	Hundley
Blackborne	Dobyns	Hunter
Blackburn	Douglass	Hutcherson
Bland	Duff	Hutcheson
Boughan	Dunn	Hutchinson

Virginia Slave Births Index, 1853-1865, Geographic Supplement

Essex	Essex	Essex
Jeffries	O'Neal	Simpkins
Jesse	O'Neale	Smith
Jessie	Parker	Southard
Johnston	Phillips	Sowell
Jones	Pillsbury	Spindle
Kay	Pitts	Stokes
Latane	Powers	Taylor
Latham	Ramsey	Temple
Lathan	Rennolds	Treble
Lewis	Rice	Trible
Loyd	Roane	Tupman
Lumpkin	Robinson	Upshaw
Mace	Rouzee	Ware
Mann	Rouzie	Waring
Matthews	Rowzee	Warriner
McDonald	Roy	Warring
McGeorge	Sadler	Westmore
McGuire	Sale	Whitlock
Micon	Samuel	Whitlocke
Minter	Sandy	Williams
Mitchell	Saunders	Wilson
Montague	Scott	Wright
Mosley	Segar	**Essex/Caroline**
Moss	Seward	Brown
Motley	Sewel	**Fairfax**
Mullins	Shackleford	Adams
Munday	Shearwood	Allen
Muse	Shepherd	Allison
Newbill	Sherman	Ansbey
Noel	Showard	Ashford

Virginia Slave Births Index, 1853-1865, Geographic Supplement

Fairfax	Fairfax	Fairfax
Ayre	Dulany	Jewell
Barker	Dulin	Johnson
Barnes	Dye	Johnston
Bates	Elam	Jones
Beckwith	Ellzey	Kidwell
Botts	Fairfax	Kincheloe
Bourbour	Farr	Leachman
Broders	Fisher	Lee
Brooks	Fitzhugh	Leigh
Brush	Follin	Lemoin
Burke	Foote	Love
Butler	Ford	Lowe
Carper	Fox	Mackall
Chapman	Freeman	Mann
Chichester	Fry	Marders
Clark	Gooding	Marshall
Coffer	Green	Mason
Coffey	Grigsby	McCrea
Coleman	Gunnell	Millan
Compton	Hall	Mills
Cook	Henderson	Milstead
Cooksey	Higgs	Moore
Craven	Hoag	Moss
Dandridge	Hooe	Nevitt
Daniel	Hove	Newman
Darne	Howard	Orrison
Davis	Hunter	Padgett
Day	Hutchison	Potter
DeBell	Hutton	Powell
Dodson	Jackson	Ratcliffe

Virginia Slave Births Index, 1853-1865, Geographic Supplement

Fairfax	Fairfax	Fauquier
Reid	Violett	Bayley
Rigg	Washington	Beale
Rouzee	Watkins	Beckham
Rowzee	Weir	Bennett
Saffer	Whaley	Benton
Sangster	Willcoxon	Bernard
Scote	Windser	Beverley
Scott	Woodyard	Beverly
Selecman	Wrenn	Bice
Shreve	**Fauquier**	Bise
Simpson	Adams	Bispham
Skidmore	Allan	Blackmore
Smith	Allen	Blackwell
Smoot	Ambler	Blight
Stewart	Anderson	Blithe
Stone	Ares	Bolen
Stuart	Armstead	Bolin
Sweeny	Ash	Bolling
Swink	Ashby	Boswell
Taylor	Ashton	Boteler
Territt	Ayres	Botts
Thomas	Bailey	Bowen
Thompson	Baily	Bower
Thornton	Baker	Bowers
Thrift	Baley	Bowie
Throckmorton	Ball	Bragg
Trott	Barber	Brent
Turley	Bartlett	Briggs
Utterback	Bashaw	Brook
Vanhorn	Bastable & Hunton	Brooke

Virginia Slave Births Index, 1853-1865, Geographic Supplement

Fauquier	Fauquier	Fauquier
Brookes	Comb	Dulaney
Brooks	Combs	Dulany
Brown	Cooper	Duncan
Buckner	Coppage	Dunham
Burgess	Corban	Eastham
Burrows	Corder	Edmonds
Byrne	Cornwell	Edmonis
Campbell	Craig	Edmons
Carnall	Crain	Edwards
Carr	Creel	Elgin
Carroll	Crittendon	Ellis
Carter	Crump	Embrey
Carver	Cummings	Embry
Catlett	Cummins	Eskridge
Chapalier	Curlett	Eustece
Chapman	Davis	Eustice
Chappelear	Dawson	Evans
Childs	Day	Fant
Chiles	DeButts	Feagans
Chinn	Detherage	Ferguson
Chunn	Diggen	Ficklin
Claggett	Diggs	Fickling
Clopton	Dixon	Field
Cochran	Dodd	Fields
Cocke	Dougherty	Finks
Cockerell	Dowell	Fishback
Cockrell	Downing	Fisher
Colbert	Downman	Fitzgerald
Colvert	Downmann	Fitzhugh
Colvin	Downs	Fletcher

Virginia Slave Births Index, 1853-1865, Geographic Supplement

Fauquier	**Fauquier**	**Fauquier**
Florance	Gordon	Henderson
Foley	Gray	Henry
Foote	Grayson	Herndon
Forbes	Green	Hickerson
Forbs	Greer	Hicks
Foster	Griffith	Hickson
Fowke	Guest	Hirst
Fox	Hackley	Hoard
Fraisior	Hackwell	Hoffman
Franklin	Hale	Hoge
Frasier	Hall	Holmes
Freeman	Hamilton	Holtzclaw
French	Hanly	Homer
Furguson	Hansberry	Hooe
Furr	Hansborough	Hope
Gaines	Hansbrough	Hord
Gale	Hansburry	Horner
Garnett	Harding	Howdershell
Garrett	Harrison	Hume
Gaskins	Hart	Humphrey
George	Hartman	Humphreys
Gibson	Hatahway	Hunton
Gish	Hatcher	Hutcherson
Gist	Hathaway	Hutcheson
Glascock	Hawley	Hutchinson
Glasscock	Hawly	Jackson
Goode	Heflin	James
Goodman	Helm	Jeffries
Goodwan	Helmes	Jennings
Goodwin	Hemington	Johnson

Virginia Slave Births Index, 1853-1865, Geographic Supplement

Fauquier	Fauquier	Fauquier
Jolly	Martin	Noland & Cochran
Jones	Mathews	Norris
Keith	Matthews	Nutt
Kelly	McCarty	Ogilvie
Kemper	McClanahan	Oglevie
Kenser	McCormick	Oglivie
Kercheval	McCoy	Oliver
Kerfoot	McGuire	O'Rear
Kincheloe	McIntier	Osburn
Kirchevill	McLearen	Owens
Kirchwell	McQuire	Padgett
Klipstein	Meredith	Page
Klipsteine	Middleton	Palmer
Klipstine	Minter	Parrott
Lacey	Mitchell	Patterson
Lake	Moffitt	Payne
Latham	Moore	Pearce
Laws	Moorhead	Peters
Lee	Morehead	Peyton
Lewis	Morgan	Phillips
Lindsey	Morris	Pickett
Loughborough	Morrison	Pierce
Loughbrough	Morrow	Pilcher
Love	Mosley	Pollock
Lunceford	Mountjoy	Porter
Lunsford	Moxley	Preast
Lynn	Murphy	Priest
Macrae	Murray	Primm
Maddux	Nelson	Ralls
Marshall	Noland	Ramey

Virginia Slave Births Index, 1853-1865, Geographic Supplement

Fauquier	Fauquier	Fauquier
Randall	Shaw	Thomas
Randolph	Short	Thompkins
Ransdell	Shumate	Thompson
Read	Sinclair	Thorn
Rector	Singleton	Tibbs
Redd	Skinker	Timberlake
Reed	Skinner	Tompkins
Reid	Smarr	Tongue
Rice	Smith	Triplett
Ricketts	Snoots	Tulloss
Rixey	Snout	Turner
Robinson	Stephens	Tyler
Rogers	Stephenson	Utterback
Rollins	Stewart	Vass
Rose	Stone	Walden
Routt	Stoven	Wallace
Royal	Stribling	Waller
Royall	Stringfellow	Walton
Rust	Strother	Ward
Sampson	Sudduth	Warder
Saunders	Sullivan	Warters
Scandland	Summers	Waters
Scanland	Sutton	Weaver
Scott	Swart	Weedon
Seaton	Taliaferro	Welch
Settle	Tapp	Welsh
Shackelford	Taylor	White
Shackleford	Tebbs	Whiting
Shacklett	Templeman	Wigfield
Sham	Thom	Williams

Virginia Slave Births Index, 1853-1865, Geographic Supplement

Fauquier
- Williamson
- Wines
- Withers
- Wood
- Woodward
- Woolf
- Woolfe
- Wright
- Yeatman
- Yerby

Fauquier/Loudoun
- Dulaney

Fauquier/Rappahannock
- Brown

Floyd
- Aldridge
- Banks
- Bishop
- Brammer
- Cannaday
- Casey
- Conner
- Cox
- Dillon
- Dobyns
- Ferguson
- Franklin
- Graham
- Griffith
- Guerrant

Floyd
- Helms
- Howard
- Howell
- Howery
- Hown
- Huff
- Hundley
- Hylton
- Kelly
- Kilterman
- Kitterman
- Lawrence
- Lesueur
- Literal
- Litterall
- Martin
- Moore
- Mosely
- Phillips
- Saunders
- Shelor
- Souder
- Sowder
- Stimson
- Sumner
- Weaver
- Wells
- Wever
- Wygal
- Yearout

Floyd/Franklin
- Ingram

Floyd/Patrick
- Graham

Fluvanna
- Adams
- Allan
- Allegre
- Allegree
- Alvis
- Anderson
- Appleberry
- Applebury
- Argyle
- Ashlin
- Ashlin & Stillman
- Bagby
- Baker
- Banks
- Bashaw
- Baskett
- Beck
- Bell
- Black
- Bledsoe
- Boston
- Boswell
- Bowles
- Bragg
- Bramham
- Branham

Fluvanna	Fluvanna	Fluvanna
Brent	Duggins	Griffin
Brooks	Duncan	Haden
Bruce	Easter	Hall
Bryan	Eastin	Hamilton
Bryant	Emey	Hamner
Buckley	Erney	Harden
Bugg	Erny	Harlow
Bulkley	Estes	Harlowe
Bullock	Estis	Harman
Bunch	Farrar	Harris
Burnley	Fisher	Herndon
Busby	Flanagan	Hodgson
Campbell	Flannagan	Holeman
Carrington	Fleming	Holland
Champion	Fontaine	Houchens
Chewning	Foster	Howard
Chiles	Fox	Huckstep
Clark	Fuqua	Hudson
Clarke	Furbush	Hughes
Clegg	Galt	Humphrey
Cleveland	Gay	Hunter
Cocke	George	Irving
Cole	Gillaspie	Jackson
Creasy	Gillespie	Jennings
Currier	Gillispie	John
Daniel	Glass	Johnson
Davis	Gooch	Jones
Doggett	Goodman	Kent
Dolin	Grant	Key
Downman	Gray	Kidd

Virginia Slave Births Index, 1853-1865, Geographic Supplement

Fluvanna	Fluvanna	Fluvanna
King	Napolean	Shiflett
Lambert	Nicholson	Smith
Lane	Noel	Snead
Layne	Norvell	Snoddy
Lewis	Omohundro	Staples
Lilley	Oppenhamer	Staton
Lilly	Pace	Stillman & Ashlin
Little	Page	Stone
Lobban	Parish	Strange
Locker	Parrish	Stratton
Loving	Payne	Tally
Lucado	Perkins	Thomas
Madison	Pettit	Thrift
Mallory	Phillips	Tinsley
Marks	Piers	Tompkins
Massie	Pleasants	Toney
Mathews	Porter	Trevillian
Matthew	Price	Trevillion
Matthews	Rey	Turner
Mayo	Richardson	Tutwiler
McCary	Robertson	Vest
McCaul	Robinson	Walker
McGehee	Ross	Webb
Melton	Ryals	Wells
Miller	Sadler	Wheeler
Modena	Sclater	White
Moon	Scott	Whitescarver
Morris	Scruggs	Will
Mosby	Seay	Williams
Moss	Shepherd	Willis

Virginia Slave Births Index, 1853-1865, Geographic Supplement

Fluvanna	Franklin	Franklin
Wills	Arington	Brooks
Wilson	Arrington	Brown
Wingfield	Arthur	Burrell
Winn	Ashworth	Burroughs
Winston	Ayers	Burwell
Wood	Ayres	Bush
Woodson	Baker	Calaway
Woodward	Barrow	Caliway
Wooling	Basham	Callaway
Woollin	Bausman	Calloway
Woolling	Beard	Campbell
Wrenn	Becker	Canaday
Wright	Beckner	Cannaday
Fluvanna/Albemarle	Belcher	Cannady
Harris	Bell	Canniday
Johnson	Bennett	Carper
Fluvanna/Buckingham	Bernard	Carter
Weir	Blankenship	Catlett
Fluvanna/Louisa	Bond	Chambers
Garnett	Bondurant	Chewning
Franklin	Boon	Childress
Abshire	Booth	Chitwood
Adams	Boswell	Choice
Akers	Bottoms	Claiborne
Allen	Bowman	Clayton
Anderson	Bowsman	Claytor
Andrews	Bowyer	Clement
Angle	Boys	Cobbs
Anglin	Bridges	Cook
Argenbright	Bright	Coope

Franklin	Franklin	Franklin
Cooper	Edwards	Hairston
Craghead	English	Hale
Craig	Fergerson	Hall
Craighead	Fergurson	Hancock
Creaghead	Ferguson	Hankins
Creed	Finney	Hannabass
Criag	Finny	Harper
Crump	Fishban	Hatcher
Crumpecker	Fishbourne	Hay
Cunningham	Fishburn	Haynes
David	Fisher	Helm
Davis	Folly	Helms
Dent	Fowler	Heptinstall
Dickenson	Frailin	Hill
Dickerson	Fralin	Hland
Dickeson	Frith	Hodges
Dickinson	Furgerson	Holland
Dickison	Furgesson	Hollond
Dillard	Garrett	Hopkins
Dillion	Gilbert	Houseman
Divers	Glaspie	Housman
Draper	Goggin	Hoy
Dratee	Goode	Huff
Drewry	Gray	Hugh
Dudley	Green	Hughs
Dunman	Greer	Hunt
Dunnings	Griffith	Hurt
Eads	Guerrant	Hutcherson
Eddes	Gusler	Hutchinson
Edds	Guster	Hutchison

Virginia Slave Births Index, 1853-1865, Geographic Supplement

Franklin	Franklin	Franklin
Hutts	Law	Moir
Ingram	Lee	Montcrief
Ingrim	Leftwich	Moore
Ingrum	Lemon	Moorman
Irvine	Lemons	Mullins
James	Leseuer	Murphy
Janny	Lesueur	Muse
Jefferson	Lipscomb	Nacolin
Jeter	Love	Nelson
Jimerson	Lovell	Newbil
Jimeson	Lumsden	Newbill
Jimison	Lynch	Niblet
Jimmerson	Machenheimer	Niblett
Jimmison	Mansfield	Nobles
Johnson	Martin	Noell
Jones	Mason	Nowlin
Jopling	Mattox	Odineal
Kasey	McCall	Palmer
Keen	McGee	Palmore
Kennett	McGhee	Pannell
Kesler	McGuire	Parker
Kidd	Meador	Pasle
King	Meadors	Pasley
Kink	Meadow	Patterson
Kinsey	Meadows	Pearson
Kirk	Menefee	Pelter
Lapred	Menifee	Perdie
Lasure	Mews	Perdue
Lavendar	Miller	Peters
Lavinder	Mitchell	Pickard

Virginia Slave Births Index, 1853-1865, Geographic Supplement

Franklin	Franklin	Franklin
Pincard	Robinson	Tench
Pinchard	Ross	Thompson
Pinckard	Rucker	Thornton
Pinckord	Saint Clair	Tinch
Pinkard	SaintClair	Tinsley
Poindexter	Sample	Toney
Pollard	Sanderson	Turnbull
Posby	Saunders	Turner
Potter	Scott	Tyree
Powell	Semones	Utly
Preston	Showalter	Wade
Price	Simmons	Waid
Prillaman	Simon	Walker
Prilliman	Simpson	Ward
Prunty	Sims	Warren
Pruntz	Smith	Webb
Pullin	Southall	Webster
Punty	Stachan	White
Pyrant	Standley	Williams
Radford	Standly	Williamson
Rakes	Stanly	Willis
Ramsey	Starkey	Wingfield
Rease	Steagall	Witcher
Reese	Stegall	Wood
Reynolds	Steward	Wooding
Richards	Stocton	Woods
Richardson	Stone	Woody
Ridgeway	Taliaferro	Wray
Ridgway	Talliaferro	Wright
Robertson	Taylor	Wysong

Virginia Slave Births Index, 1853-1865, Geographic Supplement

Franklin	Frederick	Frederick
Young	Giffin	Mason
Zeglar	Gilkerson	Massie
Zeigler	Gilkeson	Mathews
Zentmeyer	Glass	McCoole
Frederick	Hall	McGruder
Ash	Hamilton	McKowan
Baker	Hauck	McKowen
Bartlett	Headly	Miller
Brinker	Henning	Monroe
Campbell	Hetrick	Muse
Carper	Hill	Newcome
Carson	Hite	Newcomer
Carter	Holliday	Owen
Cartmell	Hollingsworth	Pifer
Chamberlain	Hucks	Powell
Chamberlina	Jackson	Pritchard
Chrisman	Jobe	Richard
Christman	Johnson	Richards
Cooley	Joliffe	Rinker
Cooly	Jones	Rodgers
Cupp	Kemp	Rogers
Danner	Kile	Russell
Davis	Kill	Rust
Day	Kite	Shane
Farmer	Knight	Shawl
Finley	Leary	Shull
Frasher	Long	Sibert
Gantt	Lupton	Silver
Garnet	Magill	Silvers
Garrett	Marker	Smith

Virginia Slave Births Index, 1853-1865, Geographic Supplement

Frederick	Fredericksburg	Fredericksburg
Stackhouse	Buck	Goodloe
Stephens	Bunnell	Goodrich
Stephenson	Burnard	Goodrick
Stevens	Caldwell	Goodwin
Stickley	Cannay	Gorden
Stickly	Carmichael	Gordon
Stine	Carter	Gravatt
Stump	Chandler	Grotz
Sylver	Cheek	Hamilton
Timberlake	Clay	Hansford
Triplett	Coakley	Hart
Turner	Collins	Hoomes
Washington	Conway	Houcey
Wotring	Cox	Hurt
Wright	Crump	Jackson
Wroten	Curtis	Johnston
Fredericksburg	Dangerfield	Jones
Alec	Deckey	Little
Alexander	Doggett	McGuire
Allen	Ellis	Mister
Ball	Eskridge	Phillips
Barton	Eustece	Richards
Berry	Fitzhugh	Roberts
Bohannon	Fleet	Rothrock
Bradley	Forbes	Rowe
Braxton	Ford	Samuel
Bray	French	Scott
Broaddus	Garnett	Slaughter
Brown	Garrett	Smith
Browne	Genther	Speed

Virginia Slave Births Index, 1853-1865, Geographic Supplement

Fredericksburg	Giles	Giles
Steady	Criner	Peck
Stephens	Crocket	Pendleton
Stevens	Crockett	Price
Stone	Dennis	Robinett
Temple	Dills	Shannon
Thornton	Douthat	Shaon
Timberlake	Duncan	Snidow
Walker	Easley	Straley
Wallace	Eggleston	Weisendonck
Waller	Ellis	Wohlford
Warren	French	**Giles/Charlotte**
Warwick	Grigsby	Morton
Waters	Guy	**Giles/Pulaski**
Wellford	Hale	Eaton
Wilson	Hall	**Gloucester**
Wroten	Hare	Acra
Young	Harman	Adams
Fredericksburg/Richmond	Hoge	Aherron
Cannay	Huffman	Anderson
Doggett	Hunter	Armistead
Fredericksburg/Spotsylvania	Johnston	Backhouse
Smith	King	Banks
Giles	Lybrook	Barron
Adair	McClaugherty	Bayne
Allen	Miller	Baytop
Bane	Moore	Bentley
Carr	Morton	Billups
Cecil	Mustard	Bland
Chapman	Pack	Booth
Charlton	Payne	Bridges

Virginia Slave Births Index, 1853-1865, Geographic Supplement

Gloucester	Gloucester	Gloucester
Broaddus	Dobson	Heywood
Brooks	Dodson	Hibble
Brown	Donevan	Hobday
Bryan	Donivan	Hogg
Burke	Dunford	Hord
Burton	Dunn	Howard
Byrd	Dutton	Hudgins
Camp	Duvall	Hudnall
Campbell	Eastwood	Hughes
Cary	Ells	Jarva
Catlett	Enos	Jarvis
Chapman	Estwood	Johnston
Chewning	Fary	Jones
Clarke	Field	Kemp
Clayton	Fitzhugh	Lane
Claytor	Fleming	Lawson
Clopton	Fletcher	Leavit
Cluverius	Flood	Leigh
Coleman	Fox	Lewellen
Cooke	Freeman	Mann
Corr	Garland	Marchant
Crump	Gibbs	Martin
Curry	Glenn	Massey
Curtis	Godfrey	Medlicot
Dabney	Graves	Medlicott
Davies	Gray	Miller
Davis	Griffin	Minor
Deans	Hall	Montague
Diggs	Hayes	Moore
Dixon	Healy	Newcomb

Virginia Slave Births Index, 1853-1865, Geographic Supplement

Gloucester	Gloucester	Gloucester
Nicolsen	Smith	Wilson
Nicolson	Smyth	Wyndham
Oliver	Soles	Yeatman
Page	South	**Gloucester/Middlesex**
Perrin	Spindle	Bland
Pointer	Stevens	**Goochland**
Powers	Stubblefield	Adams
Puller	Stubbs	Adkins
Purcell	Summerson	Agee
Rayfield	Tabb	Allan
Reade	Taliaferro	Allen
Reede	Taylor	Alvis
Riles	Teagle	Anderson
Roan	Thomas	Archer
Roane	Thompson	Argyle
Robins	Thornton	Ayres
Rowe	Thrift	Barret
Roy	Thruston	Barrett
Royston	Thurston	Bell
Scanlin	Travillian	Bolling
Sears	Trivillian	Bowles
Seawell	Vaughan	Bradshaw
Selden	Vaughn	Branch
Shackelford	Walker	Breedwell
Sheppard	Ward	Britt
Shield	Ware	Brockenbrough
Simcos	Watlington	Brooking
Simmons	White	Brooks
Sinclair	Wiatt	Brown
Singleton	Williams	Budwell

Virginia Slave Births Index, 1853-1865, Geographic Supplement

Goochland	Goochland	Goochland
Burruss	Dudley	Hatcher
Carter	Duggins	Hawkins
Cheatwood	Duke	Heath
Clarke	Duval	Henly
Cocke	Elliott	Herndon
Coles	Ellis	Hicks
Collins	Ferguson	Hobson
Colman	Finch	Hodgson
Cosby	Fisher	Holland
Cottrell	Fleet	Hollins
Cox	Fleming	Holman
Cragwall	Fontaine	Hopkins
Cragwell	Ford	Horner
Crawford	Frith	Houchens
Cross	Gathright	Houchins
Crouch	George	Hoye
Crump	Goode	Hudson
Crutchfield	Goodman	Hulsher
Dabney	Gray	Hunter
Davenport	Groom	Hyde
Davis	Guerrant	Isbell
Deane	Guy	Jackson
Deibrick	Haden	James
Deitrick	Hall	Jennings
Denton	Hamilton	Johnson
Dickenson	Hanes	Jordan
Dickerson	Harris	Kean
Dickinson	Harrison	Kedman
Dietrick	Hart	Key
Drumwright	Haskins	Lacy

Virginia Slave Births Index, 1853-1865, Geographic Supplement

Goochland	Goochland	Goochland
Lawrence	Page	Saunders
Leake	Parrish	Sclater
Lewis	Payne	Seay
Lightner	Peers	Seddon
Lindsay	Pemberton	Selden
Logan	Perkins	Shelton
Long	Phillips	Shepherd
Mahanes	Pickett	Shields
Mallory	Pleasants	Shoemaker
Martin	Poor	Shultice
Mason	Poore	Singleton
Massie	Pope	Skipwith
Matthews	Powell	Skipworth
Mayo	Powers	Smith
McGahee	Pratt	Snead
McGehee	Pryer	Southworth
Miller	Pryor	Spicer
Mills	Puryear	Stanard
Mims	Ragland	Sutton
Mitchell	Redford	Talley
Montiero	Reeves	Tate
Morris	Richardson	Taurman
Morrison	Rock	Taylor
Morson	Royster	Terry
Nicholas	Rutherfoord	Thomas
Nolley	Rutherford	Thompson
Nuchols	Salmon	Thornton
Nuckolls	Sampson	Thurman
Nuckols	Sanderson	Thurston
Pace	Satterwhite	Tilman

Virginia Slave Births Index, 1853-1865, Geographic Supplement

Goochland	Goochland	Grayson
Tinsley	Winston	Jackson
Toler	Wood	Jennings
Tredway	Woodson	Jones
Trent	Woodward	Lester
Trevilian	Worsham	Manser
Trice	Wright	Mauser
Turner	Wyer	McCarell
Turpin	**Goochland/Richmond**	Mitchell
Valentine	Trent	Osborn
Vashon	**Grayson**	Pack
Vaughan	Bartlett	Parsons
Waddy	Blair	Phipps
Wade	Bobbitt	Phips
Walder	Bourn	Porter
Walker	Bryant	Privett
Walton	Carson	Pugh
Ware	Cox	Reeves
Warwick	Curren	Reives
Watkins	Currin	Waugh
Webb	Dickenson	Young
Webber	Dickey	**Greene**
Webster	Dicky	Almond
Weiseger	Floyd	Ansell
Weisiger	Fulton	Beazley
Wight	Garrison	Bickers
Wilkerson	Gentry	Bingham
Wilkinson	Hale	Blakey
Wilshire	Hampton	Booten
Wilson	Hash	Booton
Wiltshire	Isome	Bradford

Greene	Greene	Greene
Breeding	Garth	Page
Brown	Gentry	Parrott
Buckner	Gilbert	Payne
Burnley	Goodall	Piper
Burton	Graham	Plunkett
Carpenter	Graves	Powell
Chapman	Grayson	Price
Cole	Hall	Pritchett
Collins	Harris	Richards
Conway	Harrison	Riddle
Cox	Henry	Rouzee
Crawford	Henshaw	Rouzy
Crow	Herndon	Rowsey
Davis	Houseworth	Rowzie
Deane	Hoy	Rucker
Diggen	Jarrell	Runkle
Diggs	Kennedy	Sampson
Douglass	Keysayer	Sandridge
Dulaney	Keyseear	Shearman
Dulany	Kusair	Shelton
Dunn	Malone	Shotwell
Durrett	Mayer	Simms
Early	McMullan	Sims
Eddins	McMullen	Sorrille
Estes	Melone	Southard
Fink	Miller	Stephens
Finks	Mills	Taliafero
Fishback	Munday	Taliaferro
Fitzhugh	Offield	Taylor
Fretwell	Ogg	Teel

Greene	Greensville	Greensville
Thornton	Briggs	Goodrich
Twyman	Brown	Goodwyn
Walker	Browne	Grigg
Watson	Buford	Hall
Webb	Cate	Harris
White	Cato	Harris & Murfee
Williams	Caudle	Harrison
Wood	Chambliss	Harville
Wright	Charlton	Harwell
Yowell	Clark	Heath
Greene/Albemarle	Clarke	High
Garth	Cole	Hobbs
Greene/Fauquier	Collier	Hogwood
Shearman	Cook	Howell
Greene/Madison	Crump	Jarratt
Parrott	Darden	Johnson
Greensville	Davis	Johnston
Allen	Duane	Jones
Avent	Dunn	Jordan
Bailey	Dupree	Land
Baily	Epps	Lanier
Barham	Feild	Lifsey
Batte	Fergerson	Lucas
Bendall	Ferguson	Lundy
Bennett	Field	Maclin
Birdsong	Flythe	Mason
Blunt	Ford	Miles
Branscomb	Foster	Mitchell
Branscome	Fox	Moore
Brewer	Furgerson	Moss

Virginia Slave Births Index, 1853-1865, Geographic Supplement

Greensville	Greensville	Halifax
Murfee & Harris	Turner	Adkisson
Murfree	Vaughn	Alexander
Myrick	Vick	Allen
Pair	Walker	Anderson
Pegram	Walton	Anderton
Person	Wardlow	Andrews
Porch	Watkins	Angle
Potts	Weaver	Arendale
Powell	Welton	Arendall
Prince	White	Argyle
Raney	Whitehorn	Armistead
Reese	Williamson	Armstead
Richardson	Wilson	Arnett
Robinson	Winfield	Arnold
Scott	Wingfield	Arrendall
Simms	Wood	Averett
Smith	Woodroof	Avery
Spencer	Woodruff	Bagby
Spratley	Wyatt	Bailey
Starke	Wyche	Baldin
Stephenson	**Greensville (B in NC)**	Ballow
Sturdivant	Clarke	Barber
Sykes	**Greensville/NC**	Barksdale
Taylor	Robinson	Barley
Thomas	**Greensville/Sussex**	Bass
Thorp	Parker	Bates
Thorpe	**Halifax**	Baughan
Tillar	Abbott	Beal
Tomlinson	Adams	Bennett
Trotter	Adkins	Betts

Virginia Slave Births Index, 1853-1865, Geographic Supplement

Halifax	Halifax	Halifax
Blackstock	Cannada	Comer
Blackwell	Carden	Compton
Blane	Cardwell	Conally
Blanks	Carlton	Connally
Bomar	Carr	Connerly
Boran	Carrington	Corner
Bouldin	Carter	Cosby
Boxley	Caster	Covington
Boyd	Cecil	Craddock
Bradley	Ceiling	Crank
Bradshaw	Chalmers	Crawley
Brame	Chambers	Crews
Branch	Chandler	Crowder
Brandon	Chappell	Croxton
Breedlove	Chastain	Crump
Brewer	Chiles	Crutchfield
Britton	Claiborne	Cumby
Brooks	Clark	Cunningham
Brown	Clarke	Dabbs
Bruce	Clay	Dance
Buchanan	Cliborne	Davenport
Buckannan	Coates	Davis
Bumpass (Est)	Coats	Davy
Bunt	Cobb	DeJarnett
Burch	Cobbs	Dennis
Burton	Cole	Dews
Buster	Coleman	Dickerson
Cage	Coles	Dickey
Callaham	Collins	Dickie
Canada	Colman	Dickson

Virginia Slave Births Index, 1853-1865, Geographic Supplement

Halifax	Halifax	Halifax
Dicky	Ferrill	Gravett
Dixon	Firesheets	Gravit
Dobbs	Fleming	Gray
Dodson	Flournoy	Green
Donahoe	Foard	Gregory
Donohoe	Foe	Grubbs
Dorrick	Ford	Guthrey
Downey	Forest	Guthrie
Drummons	Forrest	Hailey
Dunkley	Foster	Hale
Dunman	Foulks	Hales
Dunn	Fountain	Hall
Durham	Fourquerean	Halliburton
Easley	Fourqurean	Hankins
Edmonds	Francis	Harris
Edmonis	Franklin	Harriss
Edmunds	Freeman	Hart
Edmundson	Garner	Hawkins
Edwards	Garrett	Haymes
Elam	Gayle	Headspeth
Eldridge	Geret	Henderson
Ellington	Gerst	Hendren
Elliott	Gilliam	Hendrick
Epperson	Glass	Hendricks
Epps	Glenn	Hightower
Farmer	Glenn (Est)	Hill
Farrer	Goodman	Hite
Faulkner	Grammer	Hobson
Ferguson	Grant	Hodge
Ferrell	Graves	Hodges

Virginia Slave Births Index, 1853-1865, Geographic Supplement

Halifax	Halifax	Halifax
Hoge	Lacks	McIver
Holland	Lacy	McMillan
Holt	Lawson	McPhail
Hopkins	Lee	Medley
Howard	Leigh	Merrett
Howerton	Lester	Merritt
Hubbard	Lew	Miles
Hudson	Lewellen	Miller
Hughes	Lewis	Millner
Hundley	Light	Mills
Hunt	Ligon	Milner
Hurt	Link	Minix
Hutson	Lipscomb	Mitchell
Hyte	Locket	Moody
Irby	Lockett	Moon
Irvine	Loftis	Moore
James	Logan	Moorefield
Jeffreys	Love	Morris
Jennett	Lovelace	Morton
Jennings	Major	Moseley
Jeter	Marable	Mosley
Jinnett	Marshall	Murphey (Est)
Johnson	Martin	Murphy
Jones	Mason	Neal
Jordan	McCraw	Neubill
Jordon	McCullock	Newbill
Jourdan	McDaniel	Nichols
Kent	McDearman	Noblin
King	McGehee	Nunelle
Kirby	McGregor	Nunnally

Virginia Slave Births Index, 1853-1865, Geographic Supplement

Halifax	Halifax	Halifax
Nunnille	Purcell	Ryland
Old	Purkins	Saterfield
Oliver	Qualls	Satterfield
Osborn	Quarles	Sawyers
Osborne	Quarls	Scott
Overby	Ragland	Seat
Owen	Ragsdale	Shands
Palmer	Ransome	Shelton
Pannell	Ray	Ship
Pannill	Reaves	Simms
Parker	Reives	Simpson
Pate	Reves	Sims
Penick	Rice	Singleton
Peters	Richardson	Smith
Petty	Rickman	Snead
Phelps	Rickmon	Sneed
Philips	Ridgeway	Sparrow
Pinchback	Rives	Spencer
Pinchbeck	Roberson	Spooner
Pinchum	Roberts	Spraggins
Pleasants	Robertson	Spragins
Plunkett	Rodden	Stamps
Poindexter	Roddin	Stampson
Pointer	Rodgers	Standley
Pollard	Rogers	Stanfield
Pool	Rowlett	Stanley
Powell	Royall	Stephens
Price	Royster	Stevens
Pringle	Rudder	Stigall
Pritchett	Russell	Stone

Halifax	Halifax	Halifax
Storr	Turbeville	Williams
Stovall	Turbiville	Willingham
Stow	Tyne	Wilson
Street	Tyree	Winn
Strickland	Vaden	Winston
Stubblefield	Vaughan	Womack
Sutherland	Venable	Wood
Sutherlin	Wade	Woodall
Sydner	Walker	Woods
Sydnor	Wall	Woody
Talley	Waller	Wootton
Tally	Walne	Word
Taylor	Walthall	Wyatt
Terrell	Warren	Yates
Terry	Watkins	Yeates
Thaxton	Watson	Young
Thomas	Watt	Younger
Thompson	Watts	Yuille
Thornton	Weatherford	**Halifax/Charlotte**
Throckmorton	West	Buster
Toot	Whit	**Halifax/Hanover**
Torian	White	Hendrick
Townes	Whitlow	**Halifax/NC**
Traynham	Whitt	Brown
Tribble	Whitworth	**Halifax/TX**
Tuck	Wilborne	Blane
Tucker	Wilbourne	**Hanover**
Tulloh	Wilkerson	Adams
Tune	Wilkins	Alexander
Turberville	Wilks	Allen

Virginia Slave Births Index, 1853-1865, Geographic Supplement

Hanover	Hanover	Hanover
Alley	Bowles	Catlin
Anderson	Boyd	Chewning
Anthony	Brackett	Chiles
Archer	Braxton	Chisholm
Atkinson	Briel	Christian
Austin	Brock	Clarke
Bacon	Brockenborough	Clopton
Bake	Brockenbrough	Clough
Baker	Brokenbrough	Coalter
Barber	Brooks	Cock
Barker	Brown	Cocke
Barlow	Broxton	Cocks
Barrick	Buckley	Coldman
Bartlett	Bullock	Coleman
Bassett	Bumpass	Cook
Baughan	Burkeley	Cooke
Baughn	Burkley	Corbell
Beal	Burnett	Corbin
Beasley	Burnley	Cordin
Benton	Burrass	Cosby
Berkeley	Burress	Cox
Berkely	Burruss	Crenshaw
Berkley	Burton	Cromer
Binford	Butler	Cross
Blair	Campbell	Crump
Blunt	Carlton	Curtis
Boaze	Carpenter	Dabney
Boren	Carter	Dandridge
Bourn	Carver	Davis
Bowe	Cason	Day

Virginia Slave Births Index, 1853-1865, Geographic Supplement

Hanover	Hanover	Hanover
Deitrich	Francis	Harris
Deitrick	Frith	Harwood
DeJarnett	Fulcher	Hatch
DeJarnette	Gaines	Haw
Dick	Gardner	Hazelgrove
Dickenson	Garnett	Hazlegrove
Dickerson	Gatewood	Hendrick
Dickinson	Gentry	Hendricke
Dillard	Gibson	Henry
Doswell	Gillman	Higgason
Drizer	Gilman	Higgenbotham
Dryer	Glass	Hill
Duggins	Glazebrook	Hogan
Duke	Glenn	Hope
Dunn	Glinn	Hopkins
Earnest	Goodall	Horn
Ellerson	Goodman	Horne
Ellett	Goodwin	Hudson
Elliott	Goulding	Huffman
England	Green	Hugh
Eubank	Grubbs	Hughes
Fisher	Guthrow	Hundley
Fitch	Gwathmey	Hundly
Fleming	Gwathney	Hunley
Foard	Hall	Hunt
Fontain	Hancock	Irby
Fontaine	Harden	Jackson
Foster	Hardgrove	James
Fox	Hardin	Jenkins
Frances	Harlow	Johnson

Virginia Slave Births Index, 1853-1865, Geographic Supplement

Hanover	Hanover	Hanover
Jones	Mantle	Nolling
Jordon	Marshall	Nolting
Kelly	Martin	Norment
Kersey	Mason	Nuckles
Kimbrough	Massie	Nuckols
King	Mathews	Nunnally
Korb	Matthews	Oliver
Kosh	Maynard	Overton
Ladd	McChesney	Page
Land	McDowell	Parrish
Lankford	McGhee	Parsley
Larry	McKenzie	Pate
Lawrence	McKinzie	Patman
Leadbetter	Meredith	Patmon
Leake	Miller	Patterson
Liggan	Mills	Pattey
Liggon	Minor	Patty
Lipscomb	Mitchell	Peace
Lipscombe	Montgomery	Perkins
Litman	Moody	Perrin
Livesay	Morris	Philips
Longan	Morriss	Phillips
Lowery	Mosby	Pleasants
Lowry	Mothdell	Poindexter
Luck	Nash	Pollard
Lumpkin	Nelson	Powers
Lumpkins	Netherland	Price
Maddox	Newton	Priddy
Mallory	Noel	Puryear
Mann	Noland	Quesenbury

Virginia Slave Births Index, 1853-1865, Geographic Supplement

Hanover	Hanover	Hanover
Redd	Spindle	Tomkins
Rhodes	Stanley	Tomlin
Richards	Starke	Tompkins
Richardson	Stevens	Trainam
Robinson	Stewart	Trainham
Rowzie	Stone	Trueheart
Royster	Street	Truheart
Ruffie	Stringfellow	Tuck
Ruffin	Strong	Tucker
Sale	Sutton	Turner
Salley	Swift	Tyler
Satterwhite	Sydnor	Tylor
Saunders	Taliaferro	Vaughan
Sayer	Talley	Vaughn
Sayre	Talliaferro	Vest
Seay	Tally	Via
Shelbourn	Taylor	Viars
Shelbourne	Temple	Wade
Shelburne	Terrell	Waid
Shelton	Thacker	Waide
Short	Thomasson	Waldrop
Sims	Thompson	Waldrope
Sitman	Thornton	Warbrittian
Sledd	Tignor	Wash
Smith	Timberlake	Watt
Snead	Timothy	West
Souder	Tinsley	Wharton
Sowder	Todd	Wheat
Spears	Toler	White
Spicer	Tomkies	Whitlock

Virginia Slave Births Index, 1853-1865, Geographic Supplement

Hanover	Henrico	Henrico
Wicker	Anderson	Bradley
Wickham	Andrews	Braxton
Williams	Armstrong	Bridgewater
Wingfield	Bagby	Briell
Winn	Baird	Briggs
Winston	Baker	Brill
Wood	Ball	Brin
Wooddy	Ballow	Brock
Woodson	Barker	Brooke
Woody	Barnes	Brooks
Wooldridge	Barton	Brown
Woolfolk	Baugh	Bullington
Wright	Belcher	Bulware
Wyatt	Bell	Bunn
Yarbrough	Benson	Burch
Yeamans	Benton	Burke
Hanover/Caroline	Bernard	Burroughs
Luck	Billups	Burton
Hanover/Louisa	Binford	Camden
Cocke	Bishop	Carrington
Cook	Blain	Carter
Wickham	Blake	Cary
Henrico	Bodeker	Cauthorn
Adams	Boisseaux	Chaddick
Aiken	Bolling	Chaffin
Aikin	Botts	Chamberlain
Akin	Bouldware	Childrey
Alfen	Boulware	Christian
Allen	Bowles	Clarke
Alley	Brackett	Clay

Virginia Slave Births Index, 1853-1865, Geographic Supplement

Henrico	Henrico	Henrico
Coates	Dickerson	Gardner
Coats	Dickinson	Garnett
Cobb	Doggett	Garthright
Colquitt	Dove	Gatewood
Conrad	Dudley	Gathright
Cooper	Duke	Gay
Cottrell	Duval	Gentry
Courtney	Ellett	Gibbs
Cox	Elliott	Glazebrook
Coyhill	Ellis	Glenn
Craddock	Eubank	Glinn
Crafton	Farrar	Goddin
Crenshaw	Fergusson	Gooch
Crittenden	Ferrell	Goode
Cross	Fisher	Goodman
Crouch	Fleshman	Gordan
Crump	Fletcher	Gordon
Cullingsworth	Folkes	Gouldin
Curry	Ford	Greanor
Dabbs	Foster	Green
Dabney	Francis	Griffin
Darracott	Franklin	Grubbs
Davis	Frayser	Gunn
Deitrich	French	Guy
Deitrick	Friend	Hains
Delaplane	Fuhring	Hanes
Deleplane	Fuqua	Hanlon
Deloplane	Furgussen	Hardy
Dew	Fussell	Hare
Dicken	Galt	Harris

Virginia Slave Births Index, 1853-1865, Geographic Supplement

Henrico	Henrico	Henrico
Harrison	Jordan	McGruder
Harwood	Joseph	McKenzie
Henley	Keesee	McNamee
Herbert	Kemp	McRae
Hicks	Kerr	Melton
Higginbotham	Kidd	Meriweather
Hill	King	Mettert
Hilliard	Kinniard	Michie
Hobson	Knight	Mills
Hogan	Kuhn & Martin	Moncure
Holland	Lawson	Moore
Holloday	Lawton	Moran
Homes	Layne	Mordecai
Hopkins	Leake	More
Horner	Leber	Morgan
Houchens	Leclear	Morien
Houchins	Lee	Morris
Hubard	Lewis	Mosby
Hubert	Liggon	Mountcastle
Hunt	Lipscomb	Mutter
Hunter	Lovenstein	Myers
Hutcherson	Lyne	Nance
Hutcheson	Lyons	Nelson
Hutchison	Martin	Nettles
Isbell	Martin & Kuhn	Nimmo
Jackson	Mason	Nuckols
Jacob	Matthews	Nunnally
Jennings	Mayo	Oliver
Johnson	McConnell	Otey
Jones	McElroy	Pace

Virginia Slave Births Index, 1853-1865, Geographic Supplement

Henrico	Henrico	Henrico
Palmore	Richardson	Stewart
Parker	Robertson	Stoors
Patman	Roper	Stores
Patterson	Rowe	Storrs
Pearce	Roy	Strecker
Pendleton	Rust	Strong
Philips	Satterwhite	Sutton
Phillips	Saunders	Sweeney
Pickett	Savage	Swift
Pilcher	Schermerhorn	Tabb
Pitcher	Sedgewick	Taliaferro
Pleasants	Semple	Tatum
Poindexter	Shafer	Taylor
Pointer	Shaffer	Terrell
Pollard	Shepard	Thomas
Porter	Sheppard	Thornley
Portewig	Shine	Thorp
Powell	Sims	Thorpe
Prentis	Sinton	Timberlake
Price	Slater	Tinsley
Priddy	Sledd	Tomlin
Puttman	Smith	Trailor
Quarles	Smoot	Trainum
Ragland	Snead	Trent
Ramsey	Sneed	Tuck
Randolph	Snellings	Tucker
Ready	Spotts	Tunstall
Redd	Staples	Tunstill
Redford	Starke	Turnley
Renne	Stephens	Tyler

Virginia Slave Births Index, 1853-1865, Geographic Supplement

Henrico	Henrico	Henry
Tyree	Winston	Barrett
Valentine	Woodfin	Barron
Vass	Woodward	Barrow
Vongronning	Wren	Bassett
Waddell	Wrenn	Bateman
Wade	Yarbrough	Bauldin
Waldrop	**Henrico/Albemarle**	Belcher
Walker	Merriweather	Boswell
Wallace	**Henrico/Caroline**	Bruton
Wallthal	Garnett	Bullard
Walthall	Saunders	Burgess
Ward	**Henrico/Gloucester**	Burnett
Ware	Ware	Burton
Warren	**Henrico/Goochland**	Cahill
Warwick	Priddy	Calloway
Watkins	**Henrico/New Kent**	Claiborne
Wells	Carter	Clanton
West	**Henrico/Orange**	Clark
White	Knox	Coan
Whitlock	**Henrico/Richmond City**	Cole
Wickham	Farrar	Craig
Wilkins	**Henrico/Williamsburg**	Curtis
Williams	Bates	Dandridge
Williamson	**Henry**	Davis
Willis	Adison	Deshazo
Wilson	Anglin	Dillard
Winfree	Armstrong	Draper
Wingfield	Athy	Drury
Wingo	Baker	Dunavant
Winn	Ballard	Dupuy

Henry	Henry	Henry
Dyer	Hodnett	Morris
East	Hollandsworth	Morrison
Eggleton	Hughes	Mullins
Emmerson	Hunt	Napier
Estes	Hylton	Nappier
Farley	James	Nicholas
Finney	Jarrott	Nicolds
Flood	Jones	Norman
Fontaine	Joyce	Nunn
France	Joyner	Pace
Frances	King	Pannill
Franklin	Koger	Pannille
Galloway	Lain	Penn
Gilly	Lamkin	Penney
Good	Law	Perkins
Grant	Lawrence	Perry
Gravely	Leak	Peters
Griggs	Lee	Peyton
Hagood	Lester	Philpott
Hairston	Lovell	Pinkard
Hamlett	Lyle	Pleaster
Harbour	Marshall	Poindexter
Hardy	Martin	Preston
Hatcher	Mastin	Price
Hay	Mathews	Prunty
Hays	Matthews	Pruty
Heard	Mills	Putzel
Herd	Minter	Pyrtle
Hicks	Mitchell	Ramy
Hill	Moore	Randolph

Virginia Slave Births Index, 1853-1865, Geographic Supplement

Henry	Henry	Highland
Rangely	Thomas	Gwin
Read	Thomasson	Hamilton
Reamey	Tinsley	Hammer
Reamy	Townes	Hevener
Reany	Towns	Kincaid
Redd	Trent	Kingead
Reid	Turner	Kinkead
Reynolds	Via	Lockridge
Rich	Wade	Marshall
Richardson	Waller	Matheny
Salmon	Watkins	Rivercomb
Scales	Wells	Ruckman
Schoolfield	Williams	Sithington
Shackleford	Williamson	Stephenson
Sheffield	Wilson	Steuart
Shelton	Wingfield	Stuart
Smith	Woodall	Waybright
Spencer	Woody	Wilson
Stanley	Wootten	**Isle of Wight**
Stanly	Wyatt	Adams
Staples	Yates	Adderson
Starlin	**Highland**	Allmon
Starling	Benson	Allmond
Stockton	Bradshaw	Andrews
Stone	Campbell	Ashburn
Stovall	Davis	Atkins
Stults	Dever	Atkinson
Stultz	Ervin	Babb
Taylor	Fleisher	Bagby
Terry	Gay	Bagnell

Virginia Slave Births Index, 1853-1865, Geographic Supplement

Isle of Wight	Isle of Wight	Isle of Wight
Bailey	Cowper	Gwaltney
Ballard	Crocker	Hale
Barnes	Cutchin	Hall
Barradall	Darden	Harriss
Barradell	Dashiell	Hawkins
Barrett	Daughtrey	Hivers
Battin	Daughtry	Hodsden
Booth	Day	Holland
Boothe	Delk	Holleman
Bourne	Dick	Hott
Boykin	Dickson	Jenkins
Bradshaw	Duck	Johnson
Briggs	Edward	Jolley
Brock	Edwards	Jolly
Bunkley	Eley	Jones
Butler	Ely	Jordan
Carr	Epps	Joyner
Carroll	Fowler	Latimer
Carson	Freeman	Lawrence
Casey	Freemon	Lester
Cawson	Fulgham	Lewis
Cefield	Gale	Lightfoot
Chalmers	Gay	Little
Channell	Gibbs	Ludlow
Chapman	Glover	Marshall
Clements	Goodrich	Mason
Cofer	Goodson	McAllister
Cook	Goodwin	Minton
Corran	Gray	Moody
Councill	Green	Morrison

Virginia Slave Births Index, 1853-1865, Geographic Supplement

Isle of Wight	Isle of Wight	Isle of Wight/Norfolk
Neblett	Spratley	Lewis
Nelms	Stallings	**Isle of Wight/Surry**
Newman	Stephenson	Goodrich
Niblett	Stott	Jones
Nock	Stringfield	**James City**
Outland	Thomas	Allen
Outlaw	Todd	Bailey
Parker	Underwood	Binns
Parr	Urquhart	Blow
Person	Vail	Boswell
Persons	Valentine	Branch
Phillips	Vaughan	Bright
Pitt	Vellines	Browne
Pleasants	Walker	Bush
Pope	Ward	Camm
Porter	Watkins	Clarke
Powell	Watson	Coke
Price	Westcott	Cole
Pruden	Wester	Coupland
Purdie	White	Cowles
Randolph	Whitehead	Curtis
Rawls	Whitfield	Davis
Reynolds	Whitley	Deal
Rhodes	Williams	Deputy
Riddick	Wills	Enos
Roberts	Wilson	Ewell
Rogerson	Womble	Farthing
Scott	Wrench	Gaddy
Shivers	Wrenn	Garrett
Southall	Young	Green

James City	James City	King & Queen
Griffin	Richardson	Atkins
Hankins	Rogers	Bagby
Harrel	Saunders	Balman
Harrell	Shellburne	Banks
Harwood	Slater	Bates
Hawkins	Smith	Beverley
Henley	Spencer	Bew
Hix	Spraggins	Bird
Hockaday	Taylor	Blackston
Hubbard	Vaiden	Bland
Hubberd	Walker	Boulman
James	Waller	Boulware
Jennings	Ward	Bowden
Johnson	Warren	Boyd
Jones	Whitaker	Braxton
Knewstep	Wilkinson	Bray
Knight	Wills	Bristow
Lawson	Wynne	Broach
Lee	Yates	Broaddus
Manning	**James City/Powhatan**	Brodus
Marston	Martin	Brook
Martin	**James City/Prince Edward**	Brooke
Meanley	Piggott	Brookes
Minor	**King & Queen**	Brooks
Morecock	Acree	Brown
Morris	Adams	Brownley
Murdock	Albright	Brumley
Peachy	Allen	Brushwood
Piggott	Anderson	Buckner
Post	Archer	Bullman

Virginia Slave Births Index, 1853-1865, Geographic Supplement

King & Queen	King & Queen	King & Queen
Bulman	Didlake	Gibson
Burch	Diggen	Goalder
Burton	Diggs	Goaldman
Carlton	Dillard	Goalman
Casey	Dudley	Goldman
Cauthorn	Dunn	Goode
Cauthorne	Edwards	Gouldman
Chilton	Estis	Gregory
Clackston	Eubank	Gresham
Clark	Evans	Guthrie
Clarke	Falconer	Guy
Clarkson	Farenholt	Guynn
Clarkston	Farinholt	Gwathmey
Clarkton	Faulconer	Gwathney
Claxton	Faulkner	Gwyn
Clayton	Faulkoner	Gwyne
Clopton	Fauntleroy	Gwynn
Collins	Ferringholt	Gyron
Cook	Finch	Haines
Cooke	Fleet	Harris
Corbin	Fleet & Ryland	Harrison
Corr	Fogg	Hart
Courtney	Fox	Harwood
Cox	Gaines	Hawes
Crittenden	Gardner	Haynes
Crouch	Garlick	Hendley
Crump	Garnett	Henley
Davis	Garrett	Henly
Deshazo	Gary	Henshaw
Dew	Gatewood	Hill

Virginia Slave Births Index, 1853-1865, Geographic Supplement

King & Queen	King & Queen	King & Queen
Hoskins	Madison	Pointer
Howerton	Mahon	Pollard
Hundley	Mann	Porter
Hutchinson	Martin	Post
Jackson	Mason	Pruetts
Jeffries	Massie	Purcell
Jones	McLelland	Purks
Kay	Meredith	Pursell
Kemp	Mill	Pynes
Key	Mills	Rew
Kidd	Minor	Richards
King	Minter	Richardson
Land	Mitchell	Richerson
Langham	Moore	Roane
Langhorn	Morriss	Robinson
Langhorne	Motley	Rose
Langum	Muire	Row
Lantanna	Mundy	Rowe
Latane	Muse	Roy
Latanna	Nelson	Ryland
Latne	Neubill	Ryland & Fleet
Lawson	Newbill	Sale
Line	Norman	Samuel
Lively	Nunn	Saunder
Longest	Oliver	Saunders
Lovely	Owens	Savage
Loving	Pemberton	Schools
Lumpkin	Pendleton	Sears
Lumpking	Philips	Seay
Lyne	Pitts	Segar

Virginia Slave Births Index, 1853-1865, Geographic Supplement

King & Queen	King & Queen	King George
Shackelford	Walton	Brocke
Shackford	Watkins	Broocks
Shackleford	Wayatt	Brown
Simcos	Wedderburn	Bruce
Simpcoe	White	Bullard
Skelton	Widder	Burchell
Smith	Williams	Burnett
Smithens	Willis	Burns
Spence	Wilson	Clanahan
Spencer	Wise	Clark
Sterling	Woodard	Clarke
Stokes	Wright	Clift
Street	Wyatt	Coakley
Sutton	Yarrington	Colton
Taliaferro	Young	Corban
Talliferro	**King & Queen/Mathews**	Corbin
Taylor	Henry	Corbon
Temple	**King George**	Cox
Todd	Alexander	Cross
Tombs	Arnold	Dade
Toombs	Ashton	Dickerson
Toomes	Atwell	Dickinson
Trible	Atwill	Dishman
Trice	Baber	Edward
Tucker	Bainbridge	Edwards
Tunstall	Baker	Fairfax
Turner	Berry	Farmer
Walden	Beven	Fitzhugh
Waldon	Billingsley	Frank
Walker	Bowen	Greenlaw

Virginia Slave Births Index, 1853-1865, Geographic Supplement

King George	King George	King George
Greer	Payne	Tayloe
Grymes	Peed	Taylor
Hall	Pemberton	Tenant
Hansford	Pew	Tennant
Hooe	Phillips	Tiffey
Howland	Pollard	Treakle
Hunter	Pomroy	Tucker
Jenkins	Porter	Turner
Johnston	Potts	Wallace
Jones	Pratt	Washington
King	Price	Weaver
Lee	Quesenberry	White
Lewis	Quisenberry	Wilkerson
Lomax	Quisenbury	Wilkinson
Lunsford	Randall	**King William**
Marshall	Redman	Abraham
Mason	Rialls	Acree
Massey	Rials	Allen
Massie	Roach	Anderson
McClanahan	Robb	Armstrong
McDaniel	Rogers	Atkins
McDonald	Rollins	Atkinson
McGinnis	Sandy	Aylete
McKenney	Scott	Aylett
McKinney	Smith	Bagby
Miffleton	Sorrell	Bagby & Gary
Moxley	Stokes	Bassett
Ninds	Stuart	Berkeley
Owens	Suttle	Berkely
Parker	Taliaferro	Berkley

Virginia Slave Births Index, 1853-1865, Geographic Supplement

King William	King William	King William
Blake	Davis	Harrison
Boggs	Deffarges	Hawes
Bond	Dillard	Haynes
Booker	Douglas	Hill
Bosher	Douglass	Hillyard
Braxton	Downer	Hogan
Brooks	Drewry	Hooper
Broun	Duval	Hoopper
Brown	Eastwood	Hutchinson
Burch	Edwards	Jackson
Burke	Ellett	John
Burress	Enos	Johnson
Burruss	Eubank	Johnston
Caldwell	Fauntleroy	Jones
Campbell	Fisher	Kay
Cardwell	Fleet	King
Carlton	Fontaine	Lacy
Carter	Foster	Latane
Chappell	Fox	Lee
Clements	Frensly	Leftwich
Coalter	Friendsley	Leigh
Cocke	Garlick	Lewis
Cooke	Garnett	Lipscomb
Corr	Garrett	Littlepage
Crow	Gary	Lukhard
Croxton	Gary & Bagby	Lumpkin
Custis	Green	Mahon
Dabney	Gregg	Major
Daniel	Gregory	Martin
Davenport	Gwathmey	McGeorge

Virginia Slave Births Index, 1853-1865, Geographic Supplement

King William	King William	King William
Mill	Robins	Toombs
Mooklar	Robinson	Trant
Moore	Ryland	Travis
Munday	Sale	Trimmer
Mundy	Samuel	Tuck
Neal	Scott	Tucker
Neale	Shadwick	Turner
Nelson	Short	Turpin
Newman	Sizer	Valentine
Nicholson	Skyrin	Viar
Norment	Skyron	Viars
Painter	Slaughter	Walker
Peay	Smith	White
Pemberton	Spiller	Willeroy
Penny	Stark	Winston
Perkins	Starke	Wormeley
Pilcher	Stevens	Wormely
Pitts	Straughan	Wormley
Pointer	Sutton	Wyatt
Pollard	Sweet	**Lancaster**
Powell	Taliaferro	Anderson
Prince	Taylor	Andison
Puller	Tebbs	Armstrong
Quarles	Temple	Bale
Redd	Terry	Ball
Redford	Thornton	Banson
Rice	Tignor	Bidkar
Richards	Timberlake	Biscoe
Rider	Tomlin	Blackwell
Roane	Tompkins	Blakemore

Virginia Slave Births Index, 1853-1865, Geographic Supplement

Lancaster	Lancaster	Lancaster
Bramham	Downman	Hubbard
Brent	Dunaway	Hughlett
Brown	Dunton	Hutching
Buchan	Edmonds	Hutchings
Bush	Edmonis	Jackson
Cabell	Efford	James
Calahan	Eubank	Jesse
Callahan	Eustace	Jones
Carrell	Eustece	Kemm
Cartar	Ewell	Kenn
Carter	Fendlea	Kesterson
Chase	Fendley	King
Chilton	Flippo	Kirk
Chowning	Flowers	Landon
Coleman	Forester	Lauson
Coppage	Forrester	Lawson
Coppedge	George	Lee
Cowles	Gibson	Leland
Cox	Gresham	Lewis
Cundiff	Hall	Lunsford
Currell	Hansberger	March
Currie	Harcum	Masden
Currin	Harding	Maston
Dalby	Hatahway	McCarty
Dally	Hathaway	McKenney
Davenport	Haynie	McNamara
Davis	Hazard	Midison
Doggett	Headly	Miller
Doll	Henderson	Mitchell
Downing	Hill	Moore

Lancaster	Lancaster	Lee
Norris	Stott	Duff
Northam	Sullavan	Edds
Northern	Sullivan	Ely
Nutt	Talley	Ensin
Oliver	Tapscott	Ensor
Pace	Towles	Ewing
Payne	Treakle	Fitts
Pendleton	Waddey	Flanery
Perciful	Waddy	Fulkerson
Percifull	Walker	Fulton
Percival	Weinberg	Gibson
Pierce	Wiatt	Habern
Pinchard	Williams	Hamblen
Pinckard	**Lee**	Hampton
Pinkard	Bailey	Hensly
Pitman	Bales	Hill
Price	Ball	Hoskins
Purcell	Barron	Jones
Ransone	Beaty	Litterell
Ridgway	Boswell	Litton
Robinson	Brittain	Livingston
Rogers	Britton	Long
Rose	Carnes	Martin
Rust & Rust	Chadwell	McAfee
Sanders	Clark	Melbourn
Saunders	Colson	Milbourne
Shay	Crockett	Miller
Simmonds	Daugherty	Minter
Simmons	Dickenson	Moor
Spriggs	Dickinson	Moore

Lee	Lee	Loudoun
Morgan	Wyrick	Benton
Morison	Yeary	Berkeley
Morrison	Zion	Berkley
Myers	**Lee/Montgomery**	Berkly
Olinger	Warner	Best
Parrott	**Lee/Patrick**	Beverly
Patterson	Pinkard	Binns
Pennington	**Loudoun**	Bitzer
Provence	Abel	Blakeley
Rasor	Adam	Boland
Reasor	Alder	Bolon
Richardson	Aldridge	Bowman
Richmond	Allen	Braden
Robinson	Allmutt	Brawner
Roller	Alridge	Bridges
Scaggs	Anderson	Bronaugh
Seggs	Arnold	Brown
Simms	Axline	Buck
Sims	Ayre	Buckner
Sleet	Ayres	Burr
Slemp	Baldwin	Burson
Spencer	Ball	Burwell
Stiff	Bartlett	Bush
Stubblefield	Beard	Butcher
Vaughan	Beavers	Callahan
Warner	Belt	Callohan
Willis	Bennett	Canning
Wilson	Benson	Carpenter
Witten	Bentley	Carr
Woodson	Bentley & Smart	Carter

Loudoun	Loudoun	Loudoun
Cassaday	Drish	George
Chamblin	Dulaney	Gibson
Chancellor	Dulany	Giddings
Chinn	Edison	Glasscock
Clagett	Edwards	Gochenaur
Clarke	Eidson	Gochnaeur
Clendening	Elgin	Gochnauer
Cockerelle	Ellezy	Gochnaur
Cockerille	Ellzey	Gore
Cockran	Enders	Gover
Cockrell	English	Grady
Coe	Fadeley	Gray
Coleman	Fadeley & Jackson	Grayson
Compher	Fairfax	Gregg
Conard	Filler	Grubb
Corbin	Fitzhugh	Gulick
Crane	Fletcher	Hale
Cranes	Foley	Hall
Craven	Fouch	Hammet
Cross	Francis	Hancock
Daniel	Frasier	Harrison
Darne	Frazeer	Hatcher
Davisson	Frazier	Hawling
Dawson	Fred	Heaton
Denham	Freed	Heffner
Dennis	Freeman	Helm
Dodd	French	Hempstone
Donahoe	Fulton	Henderson
Douglas	Furr	Herkett
Drake	Garrett	Heskett

Virginia Slave Births Index, 1853-1865, Geographic Supplement

Loudoun	Loudoun	Loudoun
Hickman	Lefever	Miller
Hicks	Leith	Mills
Hill	Leslie	Milson
Hixson	Lewis	Minor
Hodgson	Littleton	Miskell
Hoffman	Love	Moon
Hopkins	Lovett	Moore
Hough	Lucius	Moran
Householder	Luck	Morgan
Humphrey	Luckett	Morris
Hunton	Lunceford	Morrison
Hutcheson	Lynn	Moss
Hutchinson	Marlow	Mott
Hutchison	Marmaduke	Mount
Ish	Mason	Newman
Jackson	Matthews	Nichols
Jackson & Fadeley	McArter	Nixon
James	McCarty	Norris
Janney	McCormick	Oden
Jenkins	McCray	Offutt
Johnson	McDaniel	Orrison
Jordon	McIlhany	Osborn
Karnes	McIntosh	Osburn
Keen	McIntyre	Pancoast
Kemp	McNamie	Peacock
Kephart	McNealy	Peale
Kline	McPherson	Peck
Leaton	McVeigh	Perry
Lee	Mead	Plaster
Leeth	Megeath	Potts

Virginia Slave Births Index, 1853-1865, Geographic Supplement

Loudoun	Loudoun	Loudoun
Powell	Shumate	Virts
Purcell	Silcott	Waltman
Pursell	Simpson	Warnal
Pusey	Skillman	Warner
Ramey	Skinner	Watson
Ramy	Slaughter	Watts
Rawlings	Smart	Waugh
Rector	Smart & Bentley	Weadon
Reeder	Smith	Whaley
Rhodes	Spinks	White
Richards	Stringfellow	Whitman
Riticor	Sullivan	Whitmore
Roads	Swann	Wildman
Roby	Swart	Wilkinson
Rogers	Swarts	Wilkison
Ropp	Taylor	Williams
Ross	Thomas	Wilson
Rousseau	Thompson	Woods
Rozel	Thrift	Wornal
Russell	Throckmorton	Wornals
Rust	Tippett	Wright
Saffer	Turner	Young
Sanders	Tyler	**Loudoun/Fauquier**
Sangster	Tylers	Jordon
Saunders	Tylor	Matthews
Scott	Upp	**Loudoun/MD**
Seaton	Vandervanter	Belt
Settle	Vandevanter	**Loudoun/Prince William**
Shepherd	Vansickler	Hutchison
Shreve	Veale	

Louisa	Louisa	Louisa
Ambler	Buck	Coleman
Ambrose	Buckner	Collins
Anderson	Bullock	Conard
Andrews	Bumpass	Connor
Armstrong	Bunch	Cooke
Arnett	Burch	Cosby
Atkisson	Burnley	Cowherd
Bagby	Burress	Crawford
Baker	Burruss	Crew
Ballard	Butler	Crymes
Barret	Byrd	Dabney
Basset	Cammack	Daniel
Baughan	Campbell	Darnal
Beadles	Carpenter	Davis
Bibb	Carroll	Desper
Bickley	Carter	Dickinson
Biggers	Cason	Diggins
Boulware	Chambers	Diggs
Bowles	Chamblin	Dodd
Boxley	Chewning	Dudley
Boyd	Chick	Duggins
Bramham	Chiles	Duke
Branham	Christmas	Dunn
Bromley	Christmass	Duval
Bronaugh	Claybrook	Duvall
Bronough	Claybrooke	Eastham
Broocks	Coates	Estes
Brook	Coats	Faris
Brooke	Cocke	Farrar
Bruce	Cole	Fleming

Virginia Slave Births Index, 1853-1865, Geographic Supplement

Louisa	Louisa	Louisa
Fleshman	Hancock	Isbell
Foster	Hancocke	Jackson
Fowler	Hanes	Jennings
Fox	Hansborough	Johnson
Francisco	Hansbrough	Johnston
Gardner	Harlow	Jones
Garland	Harris	Kean
Garrett	Hart	Keane
Gentry	Hasher	Kennon
Gillespie	Hawkins	Kent
Gilliam	Henshaw	Kerr
Gillispie	Henson	Key
Gillum	Herren	Kimbrough
Gooch	Herring	Kuper
Goodman	Hester	Lacy
Goodwin	Hill	Lasley
Goodwin & Pendleton	Hinchey	Leake
Gordon	Hiter	Lindsay
Grady	Hoggard	Lipscomb
Graves	Holladay	Locker
Grinstead	Holland	Longan
Gunter	Hollins	Loyall
Guy	Holloday	Mallory
Hackett	Hope	Mansfield
Haden	Hopkins	Massie
Haislip	Houchens	Mathews
Haley	Hughson	Maupin
Hall	Hunter	May
Halsall	Hurt	McGehee
Hambleton	Isbel	Meade

Louisa	Louisa	Louisa
Melton	Pettus	Shelton
Meredith	Phillips	Shislar
Michie	Pinkard	Sims
Mills	Pleasant	Smith
Minor	Pleasants	Smoot
Mitchell	Poindexter	Sneed
Morris	Porter	Stanley
Mosby	Pulliam	Strong
Moss	Pullium	Swif
Nelson	Quarles	Swift
Netherland	Quissenberry	Talley
Newman	Ragland	Tally
Noel	Rennolds	Taylor
Nuckolds	Reynolds	Terrell
Nuckolls	Rice	Thomas
Nuckols	Richardson	Thomasson
Nunn	Right	Thompson
Ogg	Riordon	Thomson
Overton	Roberts	Timberlake
Parrish	Robertson	Towsey
Parrott	Robinson	Towzy
Parson	Rosser	Trevilian
Parsons	Sanders	Trevillian
Patton	Sargeant	Trice
Paxson	Saunders	Tulloh
Payne	Seargeant	Turner
Pearson	Seargent	Tyler
Pendleton	Seay	Uleyate
Pendleton & Goodwin	Shaddock	Valentine
Perkins	Sharpe	Vawter

Louisa	Lunenburg	Lunenburg
Vest	Adams	Browder
Waddy	Allen	Brown
Waldrop	Almond	Bruce
Waldrope	Anderson	Brydie
Walker	Andrews	Burnett
Walton	Arvin	Burwell
Ware	Atkinson	Callis
Wash	Atwell	Cheatham
Watkins	Avrett	Chewning
Watson	Bagley	Chumney
Webb	Bagly	Clark
West	Bailey	Cole
Wheeler	Baily	Coleman
White	Baley	Cooksey
Whitlock	Barnes	Couch
Wigate	Baugh	Coutch
Wilkinson	Bayn	Cox
Williams	Bayne	Crafton
Wilson	Bell	Craghead
Winston	Bishop	Craig
Wood	Blackwell	Cralle
Woodson	Blunt	Crawley
Woolfolk	Board	Crawlie
Wright	Bolling	Crow
Wyatt	Boswell	Crowder
Yancey	Bough	Crymes
Louisa/Hanover	Bradshaw	Dance
Dabney	Bragg	Davis
Lunenburg	Bridgforth	Day
Aberbnathy	Brooken	DeJarnett

Virginia Slave Births Index, 1853-1865, Geographic Supplement

Lunenburg	Lunenburg	Lunenburg
DeJarnette	Foster	Hawthorn
Dixon	Fowlkes	Hawthorne
Dodson	Freeman	Hazlewood
Doswell	Garland	Henderson
Dowdy	Garrett	Hendly
Dupriest	Gary	Hepburn
Dyson	Gauldin	Hick
Eanes	Gaulding	Hicks
Eaves	Gee	Hill
Edmondson	Gill	Hilton
Edmundson	Goodwyn	Hines
Elder	Gordon	Hite
Ellis	Green	Holmes
Epes	Gregory	Homes
Eppes	Gunn	Hoskins
Estes	Guy	Hudson
Eubank	Haines	Hurst
Farley	Hall	Hurt
Featherston	Hamilton	Inge
Fetherston	Hamlin	Ingraham
Figg	Hammack	Ingram
Figs	Hammock	Irby
Fitzgerald	Handy	Jackson
Flinn	Harding	Jefferson
Flippin	Hardy	Jeffress
Floyd	Harison	Jeffries
Folkes	Harris	Jenings
Folley	Harriss	Jennings
Forest	Haskins	Johns
Forrest	Hatchett	Johnson

Virginia Slave Births Index, 1853-1865, Geographic Supplement

Lunenburg	Lunenburg	Lunenburg
Jones	McKinney	Pollard
Jordan	Merriman	Ponton
Jordon	Moore	Powers
Justice	Moreman	Price
Justiss	Morgan	Pugh
Keeton	Morson	Pulley
Kennedy	Neal	Ragsdale
Kirk	Neblett	Ramey
Knight	Nelson	Raney
Laffoon	Niblett	Rany
Lambert	Norvell	Rash
Land	Ogburn	Rebeal
Lane	Orgain	Redd
Lee	Orwin	Reese
Leigh	Oslin	Rex
Lester	Overton	Roberts
Lipscomb	Pamplin	Robertson
Locke	Parrish	Rowlett
Love	Pasmore	Rudd
Maddox	Passmore	Russell
Maddux	Patterson	Rutledge
Mann	Peace	Rux
Manson	Peale	Saunders
Marable	Pearson	Scoggins
Marshall	Penn	Scott
Matthews	Perry	Scruggs
May	Pettus	Seay
McAlister	Petty	Shackleton
McCormick	Philips	Shelborne
McKiney	Phillips	Shelburn

Virginia Slave Births Index, 1853-1865, Geographic Supplement

Lunenburg	Lunenburg	Lynchburg
Shelburne	Watts	Blackford
Shell	Webb	Blair
Smith	White	Blise
Smithson	Wilkerson	Booker
Snead	Wilkinson	Brown
Spencer	Williams	Buckner
Staples	Williamson	Burch
Sterne	Wilson	Burkholder
Stokes	Winfree	Burks
Street	Winn	Calloway
Sturdevant	Wood	Christian
Sturdivant	Woodson	Clark
Swinebrood	Wooton	Crumpton
Tarry	Wootten	Davis
Taylor	Wootton	Day
Terry	Worsham	Dinwiddie
Thomas	Wrenn	Dunnington
Thomasson	Yarbrough	Early
Thompson	**Lunenburg/Charlotte**	Ferguson
Tisdale	Cole	Fletcher
Townsend	Harding	Flood
Tucker	**Lunenburg/Mecklenburg**	Gilmen
Turner	Coleman	Gordon
Vaughan	Hite	Gouldman
Walker	**Lunenburg/Nottoway**	Grimaldi
Wall	Gills	Grinnaldi
Wallace	Stern	Hamney
Ward	**Lynchburg**	Harvey
Watson	Anderson	Haynes
Wattes	Armistead	Holcombe

Virginia Slave Births Index, 1853-1865, Geographic Supplement

Lynchburg	Lynchburg	Madison
Holt	Slaughter	Bell
Horner	Statham	Berrey
Ivey	Thurman	Berry
Johnson	Tilden	Bickers
Kinnier	Toney	Blakey
Langhorne	Trible	Blankbeker
Massie	Walker	Blankenbaker
McDaniel	Waller	Blankenbecker
Meem	Warwick	Bohannon
Miller	White	Bootin
Montiero	Wilkins	Booton
Morgan	Williams	Boulware
Morris	Wills	Bouton
Morriss	Woodroof	Brown
Mum	Woodruff	Buckner
Nicholson	Wright	Burk
Norvell	**Lynchburg/Loudoun**	Burke
Otey	Wyer	Burnett
Oyler	**Lynchburg/Petersburg**	Burten
Page	Edwards	Burton
Pamplin	**Madison**	Call
Payne	Allen	Carpenter
Percival	Ambler	Cave
Peters	Aylor	Chapman
Phelps	Bankhead	Clark
Poindexter	Banks	Clatterbuck
Preston	Banks & Fink	Clore
Price	Barbour	Coal
Purvis	Barnett	Coatney
Rucker	Bates	Cole

Virginia Slave Births Index, 1853-1865, Geographic Supplement

Madison	Madison	Madison
Collins	Henshaw	McGhee
Conway	Hill	McMullan
Crigler	Hudson	McMullen
Crisler	Huffman	Melone
Daniel	Hume	Melton
Davis	Jackson	Miller
Early	Jacobs	Murray
Eddens	Jarrell	Newman
Eddins	Jones	Nichol
Ehart	Kean	Nicholson
Estes	Kemper	Nicol
Fink	Kinsey	Noel
Finks	Kirkman	Powell
Finks & Banks	Lancaster	Pratt
Fishback	Leavell	Racer
Fleshman	Leitch	Reddish
Fletcher	Levell	Reid
Ford	Lewis	Rivercomb
Foushee	Lightfoot	Roberts
Fray	Lillard	Robson
Fry	Lindsay	Rose
Gaar	Lindsey	Rouse
Garnett	Lipscomb	Sampson
Garth	Lovel	Saunders
Gibbs	Lovell	Scott
Gooding	Madison	Shepherd
Graves	Marguess	Ship
Grinnan	Marguss	Simms
Harris	May	Simpson
Harrison	McDowell	Sims

Virginia Slave Births Index, 1853-1865, Geographic Supplement

Madison	Madison	Mathews
Slaughter	Welch	Dixon
Smith	Wetherall	Dunlavy
Smoot	Whitelaw	Dutton
Sparks	Whitelow	Edwards
Sprinkle	Whitlow	Fleet
Stonesiffer	Wilhoit	Forest
Story	Willis	Forrest
Stover	Yager	Foster
Strickler	Yowell	Garnett
Strother	**Mathews**	Gayle
Swan	Adams	Green
Swann	Armistead	Guyn
Tanner	Banks	Gwyn
Tatum	Barnum	Haines
Taylor	Bassett	Haynes
Terrell	Billups	Hicks
Terrill	Blake	Hill
Thomas	Bohannon	Hobday
Thompson	Borum	Hodge
Thrift	Bramhall	Hodges
Tinsley	Brooks	Howlet
Twyman	Brown	Howlett
Utz	Browne	Hudgins
Walker	Brownley	Hunley
Walters	Brownly	James
Watson	Burke	Jarvis
Wayland	Burroughs	Jones
Weakley	Callis	Keeble
Weakly	Davis	Keeton
Weaver	Diggs	Kenner

Virginia Slave Births Index, 1853-1865, Geographic Supplement

Mathews	**Mathews**	**Mecklenburg**
Kirwan	Sleet	Archer
Knight	Smart	Arnold
Lane	Smith	Averett
Lewis	Spencer	Avertt
Lilly	Tabb	Babey
Machen	Taliaferro	Bacon
Mallory	Terrier	Bagby
March	Thomas	Bagg
Marchant	Tompkins	Baird
Mathews	Turner	Balthrop
Miller	White	Baltrhop
Minter	Wiatt	Baptist
Monghone	Williams	Barbour
Owens	Winder	Barner
Pratt	**Mathews/Portsmouth**	Barnes
Pratte	Machen	Barnett
Pritchett	**Mecklenburg**	Barron
Pugh	Abram	Basey
Ransone	Adams	Baskerville
Respass	Adkisson	Bennett
Richardson	Alexander	Bigger
Roy	Allen	Binford
Sadler	Allridge	Bing
Saunders	Almond	Blane
Shackleford	Ames	Blanks
Shepard	Amos	Booker
Shultice	Anderson	Boswell
Sibley	Andrews	Bowen
Simmons	Apple	Bowers
Singleton	Applin	Boyd

Virginia Slave Births Index, 1853-1865, Geographic Supplement

Mecklenburg	Mecklenburg	Mecklenburg
Bracey	Clark	Dobbs
Bracy	Cleaton	Dodson
Bradley	Cleton	Doggett
Bragg	Cliborne	Dortch
Brame	Cloud	Drumright
Bridee	Cole	Dugger
Brooks	Coleman	Dunhill
Brown	Conner	Dunton
Browne	Cook	Durell
Bryan	Couch	Duty
Brydie	Cox	Edmondson
Bugg	Craddock	Edmonson
Burnett	Crenshaw	Elam
Burnley	Crowder	Ellington
Burtin	Crutchfield	Eppes
Burton	Crute	Epps
Burwell	Cunningham	Evans
Butler	Curry	Ezell
Butterworth	Dabbs	Farar
Byassee	Dabney	Farrar
Cabiness	Daly	Farrer
Cannon	Dance	Farther
Carington	Daniel	Faulkner
Carrington	Danton	Feild
Carter	Daves	Ferguson
Chambers	Davis	Field
Chambliss	Deadman	Fielder
Chandler	Dedman	Finch
Chappell	Denton	Finley
Cheatham	DeVlaming	Fitts

Virginia Slave Births Index, 1853-1865, Geographic Supplement

Mecklenburg	Mecklenburg	Mecklenburg
Fitz	Haskins	Jefferson
Frear	Hatcher	Jeffress
Gafford	Hawthorn	Jeffries
Gaines	Hawthorne	Jeter
Gale	Hayes	Jiggette
Games	Hays	Jimmerson
Garland	Hedderly	Johnson
Garner	Hedly	Jones
Garry	Hendrick	Jordan
Gayle	Hendricks	Joyce
Gee	Hightower	Keeling
Gill	Hinton	Keen
Gillespie	Hite	Keeton
Gillispie	Hodge	Kelling
Goode	Hogan	Kidd
Graves	Holmes	King
Gregory	Homes	Lambert
Griffin	Howerton	Land
Grigg	Hubbard	Langley
Gwatney	Hudgins	Langly
Hall	Hudson	Largeley
Halloway	Hughes	Lee
Hanserd	Hunt	Leigh
Harden	Hutcherson	Lett
Hardy	Hutcheson	Lewellen
Harper	Hutchins	Lewis
Harris	Jackson	Loafman
Harriss	Jaimerson	Lockett
Harvey	Jargley	Loon
Harwell	Jefferies	Love

Mecklenburg	**Mecklenburg**	**Mecklenburg**
Mackasey	Nickolson	Rawlings
Maden	Northington	Rawlins
Malone	Nowel	Read
Manning	Ogburn	Reamy
Marshall	Oliver	Reekes
Mason	Overbey	Reeks
Mathews	Overby	Reynolds
McAden	Overton	Richards
McCargo	Owen	Richardson
McCutcheon	Pace	Richerson
McGuire	Patillo	Riggan
Middagh	Pattillo	Riggin
Middaugh	Pennington	Riggins
Mims	Peoples	Riland
Moody	Perkins	Roberson
Moore	Pettice	Roberts
More	Pettus	Robertson
Morsen & Sedden	Philips	Roffe
Morson	Phillips	Rogers
Morton	Piercy	Rolfe
Morton & Shaw	Pollard	Rook
Moseley	Pool	Rose
Moss	Poole	Rowlett
Nailer	Porter	Rowlings
Nanney	Poythress	Royster
Nanny	Pullam	Rukes
Nash	Pulliam	Russell
Nelson	Puryear	Ryland
Newton	Rainey	Sallie
Nicholson	Raney	Sand

Mecklenburg	Mecklenburg	Mecklenburg
Sands	Taylor	Whitice
Scott	Terry	Whittemore
Seamore	Thomas	Whittle
Sedden & Morsen	Thomason	Wilkerson
Seddon	Thompson	Williams
Seddon & Morsen	Tisdale	Williamson
Seymour	Titts	Wilson
Shanks	Toons	Wimbish
Shaw	Townes	Win
Shaw & Morton	Towns	Winckler
Sheir	Tucker	Winfrey
Shelton	Tune	Winkler
Simmons	Tunstall	Winn
Sizemore	Tunstill	Woltze
Skipwith	Turner	Wolze
Skipworth	Turpin	Wood
Smith	Tutor	Wooton
Smithson	Venable	Wootton
Snead	Wagstaff	Worthington
Sneed	Walker	Wright
Spencer	Wall	Yancey
Stembridge	Wallbro	Yancy
Stone	Walters	Yates
Stow	Waltz	Young
Swinebroad	Waltze	**Mecklenburg/Louisa**
Talley	Warren	Atkins
Tally	Watkins	**Middlesex**
Tanner	Watson	Albright
Tarry	White	Bailey
Tarwater	Whitell	Baily

Virginia Slave Births Index, 1853-1865, Geographic Supplement

Middlesex	Middlesex	Middlesex
Barrick	Coatney	Jessee
Bennett	Coleman	Johnston
Berry	Courtney	Jones
Billups	Crittenden	Kemp
Blackburn	Daniel	Layton
Blake	Davis	Ligon
Blakey	Dew	Lumpkin
Bland	Dickinson	Major
Bohannon	Eubank	Mann
Book	Evans	Mason
Booth	Fauntleroy	Mathews
Bourne	Fleet	Mickelborough
Bray	Fogg	Miles
Bristow	Games	Montague
Brooks	Garden	Moody
Browne	Gardner	Moore
Bull	Garland	Mortimer
Burk	Garrett	Nicholson
Burke	Gatewood	Nicolson
Bussick	Gresham	Northam
Butler	Gressitt	Oakes
Callis	Hackney	Oaks
Campbell	Haile	Owen
Chowning	Haley	Pace
Christian	Haly	Palmer
Clare	Harrick	Parron
Claybrook	Healy	Purkins
Claybrooke	Henly	Reveer
Clondas	Hundley	Revere
Clore	Hutchings	Roan

Virginia Slave Births Index, 1853-1865, Geographic Supplement

Middlesex	Middlesex	Montgomery
Roane	Wood	Earheart
Robinson	Woodson	Eckridge
Rowan	Woodward	Edie
Rowen	**Montgomery**	Edmondson
Rowzee	Amiss	Edmundson
Rowzie	Anderson	Eskridge
Rowzy	Bain	Faulkner
Sears	Bane	Forrest
Segar	Bare	Fowlkes
Seward	Barnett	Fowlks
Shackleford	Barnitt	Frances
Sibley	Bennett	Francis
Silby	Birchfield	Gardner
Slaughter	Bird	Gibson
Smith	Boothe	Gordan
Smither	Bowyer	Grayson
Spindle	Brown	Hagan
Stiff	Callaham	Hall
Street	Callahan	Hardwick
Sullivan	Childress	Harvey
Taylor	Christian	Henderson
Temple	Conner	Heslep
Towill	Craig	Hoge
Trice	Crocket	Howe
Vaughan	Crockett	Johnston
Walden	Currin	Jones
Walker	Davis	Keister
Ware	Douthat	Kent
Wiatt	Dudley	Kirby
Williams	Earhart	Langhorn

Virginia Slave Births Index, 1853-1865, Geographic Supplement

Montgomery	Montgomery	Nansemond
Latimer	Smith	Bartlett
Lattimore	Snider	Batten
Lee	Snidow	Batton
LeGrand	Staples	Beamon
Lipscomb	Stephens	Beane
Lipscombe	Stone	Bernard
Lucas	Stuart	Betts
Lucass	Sublett	Bidgood
Lyle	Taylor	Booth
Martin	Thomas	Boothe
McCorkle	Tinsley	Boykin
McDaniel	Wade	Brewer
McDonald	Wall	Briggs
Miller	Walthall	Brinkley
Montague	Waskey	Britt
Moses	Whitescarver	Brock
Oliver	Willis	Brothers
Otey	Wilson	Brown
Peck	Younger	Browne
Peirce	**Nansemond**	Butts
Pepper	Allen	Capps
Peyton	Ames	Carney
Phlegar	Arthur	Cherry
Pierce	Ashburn	Clayton
Preston	Austin	Cobb
Price	Babb	Cohoon
Radford	Badger	Collins
Ryan	Baines	Copeland
Shelburn	Ballard	Corbell
Shell	Barnes	Corbett

Nansemond	Nansemond	Nansemond
Council	Fannie	Holland
Councill	Faulk	Hookey
Cowling	Flynn	Howard
Cowper	Folk	Howell
Creecy	Franklin	Hunter
Cross	Freeman	Jackson
Crump	Fulgham	Jenkins
Cutchen	Fulghem	Johnson
Cutchin	Gaskins	Jones
Cutchins	Glover	Jordan
Cypress	Godwin	Keeling
Darden	Gomer	Kelly
Daughtrey	Goodman	Kiger
Daughtry	Goodson	Kilby
Dean	Gray	King
Deane	Griffin	Knight
Deans	Griggs	Langston
Denson	Grimes	Langstun
Disbrow	Hall	Lassiter
Dowdy	Halland	Lawrence
Duke	Hanneford	Lee
Dunford	Hargroves	Lester
Edwards	Harrell	Lewis
Eley	Harrill	Livesay
Elliott	Harrison	Luke
Ellis	Hatton	Mansfield
Eppes	Haws	March
Epps	Hines	Mathews
Everett	Hodges	Matthews
Everitt	Hoffman	McAlister

Virginia Slave Births Index, 1853-1865, Geographic Supplement

Nansemond	Nansemond	Nansemond
McClenny	Rawles	Whitehead
McGuire	Rawls	Wilder
Miinton	Redd	Wilkins
Milteer	Reed	Williams
Minton	Riddick	Wilson
Mitchell	Rodgers	Winborne
Moore	Rogers	Wood
Murfree	Saunders	Woodward
Murphee	Savage	Wright
Murphy	School	**Nansemond/Gates Co NC**
Nelms	Shepherd	Pinner
Norfleet	Simons	**Nansemond/Isle of Wight**
Oberry	Singleton	Pruden
Outland	Skinner	**Nansemond/NC**
Parker	Smith	Smith
Parks	Snead	**Nansemond/Norfolk**
Parnell	Spivey	Gibb
Parsons	Spratley	**Nansemond/Southampton**
Peacock	Stakes	Council
Peak	Stallings	Murray
Peirce	Sumner	**Nelson**
Phelps	Turlington	Adams
Phillips	Turner	Allen
Pierce	Tynes	Anderson
Pinner	Vaughan	Arrington
Pitt	Walker	Bailey
Porter	Watkins	Baker
Prentis	Watson	Ballew
Pruden	Webb	Beasley
Raby	Wellons	Bibb

Virginia Slave Births Index, 1853-1865, Geographic Supplement

Nelson	Nelson	Nelson
Blain	Dillard	Hubard
Blaine	Embly	Hubbard
Bowling	Emmett	Hughes
Brady	Eubank	Jarman
Brent	Eubanks	Jefferson
Bridgewater	Ewers	Johnson
Brooks	Faber	Jones
Brown	Ferguson	Jordan
Browning	Fitzpatrick	Kidd
Bryant	Forbes	Lewis
Burnett	Fortune	Ligon
Butler	Foster	Lipscomb
Cabell	Fulks	Lobban
Camden	Gay	London
Carter	Giles	Loving
Christian	Goodwin	Manley
Clarkson	Gordon	Martin
Clyne	Graves	Massie
Coffey	Halsey	Maxwell
Coleman	Hamner	Mays
Crewe	Hansborough	McAlexander
Crews	Hargrove	McClellan
Cunningham	Harris	McClelland
Damron	Hatter	McCraw
Dawson	Higginbotham	Mitchell
Denny	High	Moon
Dickey	Hill	North
Dickie	Horseley	Offatt
Dickinson	Horsley	Pamplin
Diggs	Houchens	Parish

Virginia Slave Births Index, 1853-1865, Geographic Supplement

Nelson	Nelson	New Kent
Parrish	Stevens	Apperson
Patterson	Stewart	Atkinson
Payne	Stratton	Bailey
Pendleton	Taliaferro	Ball
Perkins	Thomas	Batkins
Perry	Thornhill	Bingley
Pervis	Thurmond	Binns
Peters	Trice	Blayton
Plunket	Tucker	Bowis
Plunkett	Turner	Bowles
Powell	Tyler	Bradenham
Proffit	Waddell	Bradley
Purvis	Waddle	Brown
Read	Wailes	Brownley
Rittenhouse	Warwick	Burnett
Rives	Welch	Burnley
Roberts	White	Carter
Robertson	Whitehead	Chaddick
Rodes	Willbourne	Chadick
Rose	Williams	Chandler
Rutherford	Witt	Christian
Scruggs	Wood	Clayton
Shelton	Woods	Clopton
Shepherd	Woodson	Cooke
Shipman	Wright	Crump
Smith	**Nelson/Albemarle**	Dandridge
Snead	David	Davis
Speace	**New Kent**	Dixon
Spence	Allen	Dobson
Spiece	Anderson	Douglas

Virginia Slave Births Index, 1853-1865, Geographic Supplement

New Kent	New Kent	New Kent
Drake	McKenzie	Tunstal
Duval	Meredith	Tunstall
Duvall	Minor	Turner
Ellyson	Morgan	Tyree
Eppes	Morris	Vaiden
Farinholt	Morriss	Wade
Filbates	Otey	Waring
Fisher	Parkinson	Warring
Garlick	Parrish	Webb
Garnett	Pearson	West
Gilliam	Poindexter	White
Goddin	Rabineau	Williams
Goode	Richardson	Woodward
Green	Robinson	**New Kent/Caroline**
Hackaday	Rouse	Harris
Harman	Royster	**New Kent/King William**
Hewlet	Salter	Selden
Hewlett	Savage	**Norfolk**
Higgins	Selden	Creamer
Hill	Seymore	**Norfolk City**
Hockaday	Seymour	Adams
Howle	Shearman	Anderson
Jennings	Sherman	Andrews
Jones	Slater	Anson
Knewstep	Stamper	Bagnall
Lacy	Taliaferro	Baker
Langley	Talley	Balson
Lindsey	Taylor	Banard
Macon	Timberlake	Barnes
Martin	Toler	Baylor

Virginia Slave Births Index, 1853-1865, Geographic Supplement

Norfolk City	Norfolk City	Norfolk City
Begg	Davis	Harrison
Behan	Delaney	Hartshorn
Bernard	Dey	Hatten
Biddle	Dickson	Hatton
Biggs	Diggs	Henly
Bloodgood	Dixon	Hennenberry
Brickhouse	Dozier	Heron
Briggs	Drummond	Higgins
Brooks	Duffield	Hinton
Brown	Durfee	Hoggard
Brunet	Ely	Holt
Brunette	Evans	Hunter
Bunkley	Farant	Hurnden
Burgess	Fentress	James
Burriss	Ferguson	Jeffrey
Callis	Flannegan	Johnson
Camp	Freeman	Land
Capps	Gammon	Lee
Carnes	Gaskins	Leigh
Chamberlaine	Gordon	Lewis
Chandler	Grabern	Mahone
Constable	Grady	Mallory
Cooke	Grandy	Manning
Copes	Graves	March
Corprew	Grice	Marsh
Cowdery	Guy	Martin
Creecy	Hall	McPhail
Croel	Halson	Miller
Dalby	Harding	Milner
Davidson	Hardy	Minor

Virginia Slave Births Index, 1853-1865, Geographic Supplement

Norfolk City	Norfolk City	Norfolk Co
Morris	Tebault	Armstead
Murden	Thomas	Armstrong
Nutall	Thrift	Bain
Owens	Thurigood	Ballard
Paul	Tompkins	Ballentine
Peter	Tubb	Barclay
Pollard	Tunis	Barnes
Portlock	Tyler	Barnett
Pruden	Upshur	Barry
Reed	Vaughan	Beaton
Reilly	Waddey	Benson
Ridley	Waid	Berry
Robertson	Walke	Berryman
Searls	Walters	Biddle
Segar	Watlington	Bidgood
Seguine	Wells	Bilisoly
Shepherd	Weston	Bramble
Sherwood	White	Brittain
Silvester	Whitehead	Brooks
Simmons	Whitehurst	Brown
Simpkins	Whiting	Bruce
Spady	Whittle	Bruse
Spratley	Williams	Burriss
Stone	Woodward	Butt
Strange	**Norfolk City/King & Queen**	Cannada
Swank	Spencer	Capps
Sykes	**Norfolk City/Mecklenburg**	Carney
Talbot	Whittle	Carson
Tatem	**Norfolk Co**	Cason
Taylor	Armistead	Charlton

Virginia Slave Births Index, 1853-1865, Geographic Supplement

Norfolk Co	Norfolk Co	Norfolk Co
Cherry	Etheredge	Herbert
Cooper	Etheridge	Hichcocke
Corbell	Ewell	Hinton
Cornick	Ferebee	Hodges
Cragin	Ferrebee	Holland
Creekmore	Fisher	Holstead
Creekmur	Fisk	Hopkins
Crocker	Fiske	Hoyer
Culpepper	Forbs	Hurst
Curling	Foreman	Hyslop
Cutherell	Frederick	Ironmonger
Cuthrell	Fulford	Ives
Cuthrill	Fulfore	Jackson
Dashiell	Garrett	Jenkins
Deans	Gary	Jennings
Deford	Gaunto	Johnson
Denby	Gibb	Joiner
Dennis	Gigintrottan	Jones
Deshick	Godfrey	Jordan
Drewrey	Gray	Keeling
Drewry	Griffin	Kellam
Drummond	Grimes	Kellum
Dudley	Hall	Kilby
Duke	Halstead	Kilgore
Duncan	Hamburg	Kingman
Edwards	Hanberry	Lash
Ellis	Hanbury	Lawrence
Eskridge	Hardy	Lindsay
Eteredge	Harrison	Linton
Etherage	Henly	Lockheart

Virginia Slave Births Index, 1853-1865, Geographic Supplement

Norfolk Co	Norfolk Co	Norfolk Co
Love	Otly	Stewart
Lynch	Outten	Stoakes
Mackan	Parsons	Stokes
Mackey	Peaton	Strand
Mackie	Peed	Stroud
Martin	Perry	Sykes
McClenny	Petree	Sylvester
McClerney	Peyton	Tarrant
McCoy	Phillips	Tartt
McKan	Portlock	Tatem
McPherson	Pritchard	Taylor
Mears	Pumphrey	Tennis
Mercer	Richardson	Travis
Merchant	Ritter	Twiford
Miers	Roach	Upshur
Miles	Roberts	Verria
Miller	Robertson	Wallace
Mills	Robinson	Warden
Moore	Rose	Warren
Morris	Sammons	Webb
Munden	Sanderson	West
Myers	Scott	Weston
Nash	Seymour	Whidbee
Newbern	Shaw	White
Newby	Sikes	Wickham
Nicholas	Simmons	Wickings
Norris	Sinton	Wilkins
Northern	Sivilla	Williams
Notham	Smith	Williamson
Old	Spence	Willson

Virginia Slave Births Index, 1853-1865, Geographic Supplement

Norfolk Co	Northampton	Northampton
Wilson	Copes	Heath
Wise	Costin	Henderson
Wood	Cottingham	Holland
Woods	Custis	Horsey
Wordan	Dalby	Hunt
Wright	Dennis	Jacob
Yates	Dixon	James
Norfolk Co/Norfolk City	Doughty	Jarvis
Biddle	Downes	Johnson
Northampton	Downing	Kellam
Adair	Dowty	Kendall
Addison	Duncan	Ker
Anderson	Dunton	Kerr
Andrews	Elliott	Knight
Ashby	Evans	Leatherbury
Bagly	Eyre	Major
Bagwell	Fatherly	Mapp
Bayly	Fisher	Matthews
Bell	Fitchett	Mears
Belote	Floyd	Mills
Bowdoin	Garretson	Moore
Bradford	Garrison	Nelson
Brickhouse	Godwin	Nicholson
Brittingham	Goffigon	Nottingham
Cary	Griffin	Parker
Casey	Griffith	Parsons
Christian	Gunter	Peed
Churn	Haley	Powell
Clark	Hallett	Purnell
Collins	Harmanson	Read

Virginia Slave Births Index, 1853-1865, Geographic Supplement

Northampton	Northampton	Northumberland
Ringgold	Turlington	Allen
Roberts	Turner	Ball
Robins	Twiford	Barnes
Sample	Tyson	Basye
Satchell	Upshaw	Bates
Saunders	Upshur	Bayly
Savage	Waddey	Bayse
Scarborough	Waddy	Bell
Scott	Wescoat	Betts
Shroeder	West	Blackwell
Simkins	Wheeler	Blundon
Smaw	Widegon	Booth
Smith	Wideon	Brent
Spady	Widgen	Bromley
Stewart	Widgeon	Broun
Stoakley	Wilkins	Brown
Stockley	Williams	Brumley
Stokeley	Wilson	Burgess
Stratton	Window	Carter
Tankard	Wise	Claughton
Tatem	Yerby	Claybrook
Taylor	Young	Cockarell
Tazewell	**Northampton/Accomack**	Cockarille
Thom	Collonna	Cockerille
Thomas	Garrison	Cole
Thorn	Waddy	Coles
Thurston	**Northampton/James City**	Connellee
Travis	Nottingham	Cookman
Trehurn	**Northumberland**	Coppedge
Trower	Alexander	Corben

Virginia Slave Births Index, 1853-1865, Geographic Supplement

Northumberland	Northumberland	Northumberland
Covington	Howearth	Owens
Cowart	Hudnall	Palmer
Cox	Hudson	Pasquith
Cralle	Hughlett	Perciful
Crowther	Hurst	Pillsberry
Cundiff	Ingraham	Pillsbury
Davenport	Jett	Raines
Dawson	Jones	Rice
Dodson	Keene	Richardson
Downing	Keeve	Sampson
Edwards	Kelley	Self
Eskridge	Kelly	Shirley
Eustece	Kenner	Slocum
Evans	Kent	Smith
Fallen	Lamdell	Snow
Fallin	Lansdell	Stakes
Gaskins	Lawson	Stith
Gill	Leland	Straughan
Hall	Lewis	Sutton
Harcum	Lyell	Tignor
Hardin	Maley	Toulson
Harding	Marsh	Travis
Harvey	McClanahan	Turner
Harvie	Moore	Winstead
Haynes	Neal	Wright
Haynie	Neale	**Nottoway**
Headley	Nelms	Allen
Henderson	Noel	Alston
Hill	Northern	Anderson
Howarth	Opie	Atkins

Virginia Slave Births Index, 1853-1865, Geographic Supplement

Nottoway	Nottoway	Nottoway
Austin	Clarke	Fowlkes
Baldwin	Clay	Furgerson
Barrow	Cockraham	Furgusson
Barton	Cockrahan	Gay
Bass	Connalley	Gill
Bates	Connally	Gills
Baun	Connelly	Godsey
Beverley	Cralle	Goodwin
Beverly	Crally	Goulder
Bevill	Crenshaw	Grammar
Bland	Crump	Green
Boisseau	Davis	Griffin
Booth	Dean	Grigg
Borum	Dickerson	Griggs
Bouldin	Dickins	Gunn
Bourne	Dickinson	Guy
Bradshaw	Doobins	Hamblin
Bragg	Dyson	Hamlin
Bridgforth	Eggleston	Hardaway
Brown	Ellett	Harper
Burke	Ellington	Harris
Burton	Epes	Hart
Cabaniss	Epperson	Hatchett
Campbell	Eustie	Hawkes
Carey	Farley	Hawks
Carter	Ferguson	Hicks
Cary	Fitzgerald	Horner
Casper	Fletcher	Hudgings
Christopher	Flippin	Hudgins
Christopher (Est)	Foster	Hudson

Virginia Slave Births Index, 1853-1865, Geographic Supplement

Nottoway	Nottoway	Nottoway
Hurt	Neblett	Sydnor
Ingram	Nelson	Taylor
Irby	Newman	Thacker
Jackson	Niblett	Thomas
Jeffress	Oliver	Todd
Jeffrey	Osborn	Tucker
Jeffreys	Osborne	Tuggle
Jenings	Overton	Vaughan
Jennings	Owen	Verser
Jeter	Perkinson	Waller
Johnson	Pollard	Ward
Jones	Ponton	Watkins
Justice	Powell	Watson
Justin	Quarles	Watts
Knight	Reams	Webster
Leath	Riddick	Weeks
Lipscomb	Roberts	White
Livsey	Robertson	Wicks
Magers	Rowlett	Williams
Majore	Royall	Williamson
Marshall	Sallard	Wills
Mason	Scott	Wilson
McGuire	Shackleford	Wingo
McQuin	Shore	Winn
McQuir	Sims	Worsham
Miller	Slaughter	**Nottoway/Chesterfield**
Morgan	Sneed	Royall
Motley	Stern	**Nottoway/Springfield**
Mumford	Still	Bland
Munford	Stith	

Virginia Slave Births Index, 1853-1865, Geographic Supplement

Orange	Orange	Orange
Adams	Campbell	Estes
Alexander	Canaday	Estis
Almond	Carson	Evans
Anderson	Cave	Farish
Andrews	Chapman	Faudree
Austin	Chariters	Fitzhugh
Bailey	Charters	Fraizer
Baldwin	Chewning	Frazer
Ballard	Clark	Frazier
Bankhead	Clarke	Gee
Barbour	Cobbs	Gibson
Beale	Coleman	Goldsmith
Beazley	Collins	Goodwin
Bell	Conway	Gordon
Bickers	Cook	Goss
Blair	Cooper	Graham
Blaydes	Cowherd	Grasty
Bledsoe	Crenshaw	Graves
Bond	Crockford	Grymes
Boston	Daniel	Hall
Boulware	Davis	Halsey
Bradford	Douglass	Ham
Brockman	Downer	Hamm
Brooking	Dulaney	Hancock
Brown	Dunn	Harris
Buckner	Earnest	Hatch
Bull	Eddins	Hawkins
Bullock	Edwards	Haxall
Burrus	Eheart	Henderson
Burruss	Ellis	Henshaw

Virginia Slave Births Index, 1853-1865, Geographic Supplement

Orange	Orange	Orange
Herndon	Mansfield	Riner
Hiden	Mason	Roach
Holladay	Massey	Roberson
Holliday	Massie	Roberts
Holloday	Meade	Robinson
Houck	Mills	Rose
Houseworth	Minor	Row
Houston	Moody	Sale
Hume	Moore	Samuel
Jacobs	Morris	Sanders
Jennings	Morton	Sandford
Jerdone	Nalle	Sanford
Johnson	Newman	Saunders
Jones	Omohondro	Scisson
Jordon	Omohundro	Scott
Kannady	Owens	Siberts
Kendall	Pannill	Simcos
Kennedy	Parker	Sisson
King	Parrott	Skinker
Kinzer	Payne	Sleet
Knox	Peacher	Smith
Lancaster	Porter	Sneed
Lee	Priest	Spotswood
Lipscomb	Quarles	Spottswood
Lucas	Quisenberry	Stanard
Lucus	Rawlings	Stephen
Macon	Reynolds	Stephens
Madison	Rhoades	Stevens
Magruder	Rhoads	Stockdon
Mallory	Richards	Stringfellow

Virginia Slave Births Index, 1853-1865, Geographic Supplement

Orange	Orange	Page
Strother	Williamson	Bumgardner
Stubblefield	Willis	Buracker
Stubbs	Wilthoit	Burner
Taliaferro	Wood	Campbell
Taylor	Woodville	Carpenter
Terrell	Woolfolk	Coffman
Terrill	Woolfork	Cook
Thomas	Wright	Corbin
Thompson	Young	Deal
Thomson	**Orange (B in Albemarle)**	Dovel
Thornton	Clark	Eddins
Thrift	**Orange/Madison**	Fleming
Tinder	Jones	Flemming
Tinsley	**Page**	Fox
Towles	Aiken	Freeman
Turner	Aleshire	Graves
Vawter	Almond	Grove
Waddy	Barbee	Hershberger
Walker	Barber	Huffman
Warren	Barrner	Jett
Wayland	Beale	Jones
Webb	Bear	Jordan
White	Beazley	Jordon
Whitelaw	Beidler	Kaufman
Whitelow	Bell	Kendrick
Whitlow	Biedler	Keyser
Wigglesworth	Booton	Kibler
Wiglesworth	Brown	Kingary
Wilhoit	Brubaker	Kingree
Williams	Brumback	Kite

Page	Patrick	Patrick
Koontz	Akers	Edward
Lauck	Allen	Edwards
Lawler	Anglin	Emerson
Lionberger	Anthony	Emmerson
Long	Athy	Falconer
Miller	Ayres	Fenney
Mohler	Barnard	Finney
Moore	Barter	Flippen
O'Bannon	Bennett	Flippin
Perry	Bowling	Foley
Petty	Brammer	Foster
Pitman	Brin	France
Ponn	Brown	Frances
Price	Bryant	Gilbert
Reedy	Burnett	Giles
Ruffner	Cannaday	Gill
Rust	Carter	Gray
Sedwick	Clark	Gunter
Shenk	Cobb	Hagood
Snyder	Cobbs	Hairston
Spitler	Cochran	Hanby
Stover	Cockram	Hariston
Strickler	Conner	Harris
Strole	Corn	Hatcher
Utz	Critz	Hill
Varner	Dalton	Hines
Williams	Davis	Houchins
Wood	Dehart	Hubbard
Patrick	Deheart	Hughes
Adams	Dodson	Hughs

Virginia Slave Births Index, 1853-1865, Geographic Supplement

Patrick	Patrick	Patrick
Hulsher	Pendleton	Underwood
Hylton	Penn	Vaughan
Ivie	Pilson	Via
Jackson	Poindexter	Walker
Jarratt	Potter	Waller
Joyce	Prunty	West
Kennerly	Puckett	Williams
King	Rakes	Willson
Koger	Reed	Wilson
Lackey	Reynolds	Woodall
Lacky	Robertson	Woolwine
Langhorne	Roger	Wright
Leah	Rorer	Yates
Lee	Ross	Young
Martin	Sayars	Ziglar
McCabe	Scales	Zigler
Meredith	Shelton	**Patrick/Henry**
Mills	Simmons	Hagood
Minifee	Smith	**Petersburg**
Moir	Soyars	Alfriend
Moore	Spencer	Allen
Moran	Staples	Alley
Morris	Stone	Andrews
Murphy	Stuart	Anthony
Nowlin	Tatum	Archer
Oakly	Taylor	Atkisson
Overby	Terry	Badger
Pack	Thomas	Batte
Pannell	Tuggle	Bendall
Parker	Turner	Bishop

Virginia Slave Births Index, 1853-1865, Geographic Supplement

Petersburg	Petersburg	Petersburg
Boisseau	Costigan	Hamblin
Bolling	Cowles	Hamilton
Booth	Cox	Hannon
Bourdon	Crowder	Harmon
Bragg	Crump	Harris
Branch	Daniel	Harrison
Brander	Davidson	Heath
Brister	Davis	Hill
Broadnax	Dean	Hinton
Brown	Deaton	Holerby
Brownley	Dodson	Jackson
Burns	Donnan	Jamison
Burrell	Drinkard	Jarratt
Butler	Drummond	Jarrett
Butterworth	Dugger	Jaynes
Caimes	Eckles	Jones
Cairns	Elliott	Judkins
Camp	Ennis	Justice
Caperton	Falconer	Justiss
Carrington	Floyd	Kello
Chappill	Friend	Kevan
Charlton	Garland	Kidd
Claiborne	Gates	Leath
Clements	Glover	Lee
Cogbill	Goodrum	Lemoine
Coghill	Goodwin	Leslie
Coldwell	Goodwyn	Leyburn
Coleman	Grigg	Lunsford
Cooper	Haines	Lynch
Corling	Hall	Lyon

Virginia Slave Births Index, 1853-1865, Geographic Supplement

Petersburg	Petersburg	Petersburg
Maben	Pollard	Watkins
Mabry	Pugh	Watson
Magee	Puller	Weddell
Major	Rivers	Weeks
Maxwell	Rives	Weisiger
May	Roberts	Wells
McCullock	Robertson	White
McFarland	Robinson	Whitmore
McIlwaine	Ruffin	Whitt
Meade	Russell	Wilkerson
Michel	Simpson	Williams
Michie	Slaughter	Wills
Mickie	Smith	Witcher
Miller	Smithey	Wyatt
Minge	Smyth	Young
Montague	Snyder	**Petersburg/Dinwiddie**
Morrison	Spratley	Donnan
Morton	Stewart	Friend
Oliver	Stith	Miner
Olivier	Sydner	Minor
Orr	Sydnor	Muir
Osborne	Tannahill	Munce
Pannill	Thompson	Tuck
Paterson	Todd	**Petersburg/Southampton**
Patterson	Townes	James
Paul	Tuck	**Pittsylvania**
Peace	Turner	Abbott
Peebles	Vaughan	Adams
Penman	Wallace	Adkerson
Petricolas	Wallton	Adkins

Virginia Slave Births Index, 1853-1865, Geographic Supplement

Pittsylvania	Pittsylvania	Pittsylvania
Adkinson	Blanks	Carey
Allen	Boaz	Carlwell
Anderson	Bohannon	Carrington
Anderson & Flippin	Boone	Carter
Andrews	Boothe	Chaney
Angle	Bowe	Chappell
Angles	Bowen	Christian
Anthony	Bowling	Claiborn
Arnold	Boyd	Claiborne
Astin	Bradley	Clark
Atkinson	Bradner	Clemant
Badgett	Breedlove	Clement
Bailey	Brightwell	Clements
Baily	Brilhart	Cobb
Banks	Brodnax	Cobbs
Barber	Brown	Cocke
Barker	Brumfield	Cole
Barksdale	Buford	Coleman
Barksdale & Hall	Burdett	Coles
Bass	Burger	Collie
Bates	Burnett	Compton
Baugh	Burton	Conway
Baynes	Cabaniss	Cook
Beavers	Cabell	Cooper
Bell	Cabiness	Corbin
Belt	Cabinis	Cosby
Bennett	Callaway	Craft
Berger	Calloway	Crewes
Binford	Camorine	Crews
Blair	Cardwell	Crider

Virginia Slave Births Index, 1853-1865, Geographic Supplement

Pittsylvania	Pittsylvania	Pittsylvania
Cunningham	Emmerson	Francis
Dallas	English	Franklin
Dallis	Estes	Fuller
Dalton	Fackler	Fulton
Daniel	Falconer	Furgerson
Davice	Falkner	Gammon
Davis	Fallen	Gardner
Dawson	Fallin	Garland
Devin	Faris	Gatewood
Dews	Farmer	Gaulding
Dick	Fenlaw	George
Dickenson	Fergerson	Gibson
Dickerson	Ferguson	Gilbert
Dickinson	Ferrell	Giles
Dickson	Ferrill	Gill
Dillard	Finney	Gills
Dix	Fitts	Gilmore
Dixon	Fitzgerald	Glass
Dodd	Flippen	Glenn
Dodson	Flippin	Goad
Doe	Flippin & Anderson	Goggin
Dogan	Flippin & Hightower	Good
Doyle	Folks	Goodman
Drewry	Fontain	Gosney
Drury	Fontaine	Grant
Eanes	Fore	Grasty
Easley	Fountain	Graves
Echols	Fowler	Green
Edmunds	Fowlkes	Gregory
Edwards	Fowlks	Grigg

- 162 -

Virginia Slave Births Index, 1853-1865, Geographic Supplement

Pittsylvania	Pittsylvania	Pittsylvania
Griggs	Hightower	Kelly
Grigory	Hightower & Flippin	King
Guerrant	Hines	Kirby
Guinn	Hobson	Lain
Gunter	Hodges	Lanier
Guthrie	Hodnett	Law
Haden	Holland	Layne
Hairston	Holt	Lea
Hale	Hoofman	Lee
Haley	Howard	Leftwich
Hall	Hubbard	Lew
Ham	Hughes	Lewis
Hambleton	Hughs	Lindsay
Hamner	Hundley	Lindsey
Hampton	Hunt	Linnear
Hankins	Hunter	Linthicum
Hannah	Hurt	Lipford
Hardy	Hutchings	Lipscomb
Harper	Inge	Logan
Harraway	Inman	Lovelace
Harris	Irby	Lowry
Harroway	James	Luck
Harvey	Jefferson	Lumpkin
Hatcher	Jennings	Lumpkins
Hatchett	Johns	Lyon
Hawker	Johnson	Mahan
Hedrick	Jones	Mann
Henry	Keatts	Marshall
Herndon	Keen	Martin
Hicks	Keesee	Matthews

Pittsylvania	Pittsylvania	Pittsylvania
May	Neal	Piercy
Mayhaw	Newby	Pigg
McAlister	Noel	Plunkett
McCaffrey	Noell	Poindexter
McDaniel	Norman	Powell
McDearman	Nowell	Price
McHaney	Nunnelee	Pringle
McLaughlin	Oakes	Pritchett
Meadors	Oaks	Pullen
Meadow	Odineal	Pullin
Meadows	Ogborne	Purkins
Mece	Oliver	Ragsdale
Miller	Orander	Ramsay
Millner	Organ	Ramsey
Millnor	Owen	Redd
Minter	Pannill	Reynolds
Mitchell	Parish	Richardson
Mohr	Parker	Rison
Monros	Parrish	Roberson
Moore	Parsons	Robertson
Moorman	Pasley	Robinson
Morrison	Patrick	Rogers
Morton	Paxton	Rorer
Moss	Payne	Rover
Motley	Peatross	Royal
Murrell	Penic	Royall
Muse	Penick	Rucker
Mustain	Perkins	Samson
Myers	Petty	Sanders
Nance	Pierce	Saunders

Virginia Slave Births Index, 1853-1865, Geographic Supplement

Pittsylvania	Pittsylvania	Pittsylvania
Sayers	Sykes	Vaughn
Scarce	Tait	Venable
Scates	Tanner	Voss
Sceatts	Tarpley	Waddill
Scott	Tate	Walden
Scruggs	Taylor	Walker
Shaw	Terry	Walkup
Shelhorse	Thomas	Waller
Shelton	Thompkins	Walne
Shields	Thompson	Walrond
Short	Thornton	Walters
Shumaker	Thurman	Walton
Simmons	Thurmun	Ward
Simpson	Thweatt	Watkins
Singleton	Tinsley	Watson
Slough	Toler	Wells
Smith	Tosh	West
Snow	Towler	Wetherford
Soyars	Townes	White
Sparks	Towns	Whitehead
Sparrow	Travis	Whitney
Stamps	Tredway	Whittle
Starkey	Trent	Wier
Stepto	Trice	Wiles
Still	Trotter	Wilkerson
Stimpson	Tucker	Wilkinson
Stone	Tunstall	Williams
Stow	Turner	Williamson
Swan	Vaden	Wilson
Swanson	Vaughan	Wimbish

Virginia Slave Births Index, 1853-1865, Geographic Supplement

Pittsylvania	Pittsylvania/Staunton	Portsmouth
Witcher	Coles	Jarvis
Womack	Myers	Knott
Wood	**Portsmouth**	Long
Wooding	Anderson	Maupin
Woodson	Beaton	McRay
Woody	Benthall	Minter
Worsham	Bilisoly	Moore
Wright	Brownley	Myers
Wyatt	Butt	O'Niel
Wyllie	Carney	Outten
Wynne	Cocke	Owens
Yates	Collins	Porter
Yeatts	Cooke	Randolph
Younger	Culpepper	Riddick
Pittsylvania/Appomattox	Davis	Riddicks
Adams	Dean	Savage
Pittsylvania/Danville	Downs	Scott
Bethell	Emmerson	Smith
Buford	Foreman	Sneed
Grasty	Freeman	Talbot
Holland	Gregg	Tart
Johnson	Grice	Tatem
Johnston	Hardy	Tea
Lucas	Herbert	Tee
Millner	Hobday	Toomer
Neal	Hodges	Williams
Sampson	Hope	Williamson
Williams	Hudgens	Willy
Womack	Hume	Wilson
Wyllie	Hundley	Wonnecott

Powhatan	Powhatan	Powhatan
Abraham	Clegg	Eustece
Adams	Cocke	Fariss
Adkins	Cofer	Farley
Allen	Coleman	Faudree
Amonette	Cooke	Finch
Anderson	Cooper	Finney
Apperson	Cosby	Finny
Archer	Cox	Flournoy
Ashlin	Crostick	Forsee
Aston	Crowder	Fowler
Atkinson	Crump	Frayser
Bagby	Dabney	French
Baily	Dance	Gates
Baird	Darisson	Giles
Ball	Davisson	Gilliam
Barley	Dearan	Gills
Basley	Denoon	Godsey
Bass	Depp	Goode
Baugh	Diuguid	Goodman
Blunt	Doake	Gordon
Bolling	Dorset	Graves
Bowles	Dorsett	Gray
Bradley	Dossett	Guy
Bristow	Drake	Hancock
Brown	Dunkum	Hancocke
Browning	Eanes	Hanic
Bryant	Eggleston	Harris
Burwell	Elam	Harrison
Busby	Ellet	Harvie
Campbell	Ellett	Haskins

Virginia Slave Births Index, 1853-1865, Geographic Supplement

Powhatan	Powhatan	Powhatan
Hatcher	McCaw	Palmore
Hendrick	McCaw & Lay	Parker
Henning	McGruder	Payne
Hobson	McKenzie	Pemberton
Holman	McKinzie	Phaup
Howard	McLaurine	Pickrell
Howell	Michaux	Pierce
Hughes	Michaux & Walthall	Pleasants
Hurt	Miller	Porter
Jackson	Montague	Povall
Jennings	Moody	Powell
Jeter	Moore	Powers
Johns	Moorman	Ragland
Jones	Morrison	Robertson
Jordan	Mosby	Robinson
Justis	Moseley	Ronald
Laprede	Mosely	Royall
Lay	Mosley	Rudd
Lee	Mosly	Sampson
Leigh	Munford	Saunders
Lester	Murray	Scott
Ligon	Murry	Scruggs
Lyon	Nash	Selden
Maddox	Nelson	Seldon
Martin	Netherland	Siddons
Maxey	Newton	Simpson
Maxy	Noble	Skelton
Mayo	Old	Skipwith
McCan	Owen	Skipworth
McCann	Palmer	Sledd

Virginia Slave Births Index, 1853-1865, Geographic Supplement

Powhatan	Powhatan	Prince Edward
Smith	Watkins	Atkinson
Spears	Weisiger	Atwood
Spencer	White	Baker
Stegar	Whitfield	Baldwin
Steger	Whitlock	Barksdale
Stratton	Wilburn	Bass
Stringer	Wilkinson	Beach
Sublett	Williams	Beazley
Swann	Winfree	Bell
Talley	Winifree	Benford
Tally	Wood	Berkeley
Tatum	Woodfin	Berkley
Taurman	Wooldridge	Berry
Taylor	Woolridge	Binford
Thrift	Worsham	Blanton
Thweat	Wren	Bolling
Tinsley	**Powhatan/Goochland**	Bondurant
Toney	Archer	Booker
Trent	**Prince Edward**	Borum
Tucker	Adams	Boulton
Turpin	Agnew	Bradley
Tyree	Allen	Bradshaw
Vaughan	Allmond	Branch
Walke	Alsop	Briant
Walker	Alsup	Brightwell
Walthall	Anderson	Brooks
Walton	Armstead	Brown
Warinner	Arvin	Bruce
Warrick	Arvine	Bryant
Warriner	Atkins	Buffla Congregation

Virginia Slave Births Index, 1853-1865, Geographic Supplement

Prince Edward	Prince Edward	Prince Edward
Burk	Daniel & McGehee	Faulkner
Burke	Davenport	Flippen
Cabbell	David	Flippin
Calhoon	Davidson	Flournoy
Calhoun	Davis	Ford
Carrington	Dawson	Fore
Carter	DeJarrette	Foster
Cary	Dickerson	Fowler
Chambers	Dickinson	Fowlkes
Chappell	Dillon	Franklin
Cheadle	Drincard	Garrett
Cheadles	Dungan	Gilliam
Childress	Dungans	Gillispie
Chockley	Dunnavant	Gills
Chumbley	Dunnington	Glenn
Chumney	Dupuy	Goode
Clark	Edmunds	Gordon
Clarke	Eggleston	Graves
Cobb	Elam	Gray
Cockram	Elcan	Green
Cox	Ellett	Guthery
Cralle	Ellette	Guthrey
Cravin	Ellington	Hambleton
Crawley	Elliott	Hamilton
Crute	Elliotte	Hardaway
Cunningham	Ely	Harper
Dabney	Evans	Harris
Dalby	Ewing	Harvey
Dance	Farley	Haskins
Daniel	Farrar	Hatchett

Virginia Slave Births Index, 1853-1865, Geographic Supplement

Prince Edward	Prince Edward	Prince Edward
Helmick	Lineave	Morrissett
Hemlick	Lockett	Morton
Henderson	Mann	Moseley
Hickson	Marker	Moss
Hill	Marshall	Motley
Hilliard	Martin	Mottley
Hines	McCargo	Mottly
Hix	McCormick	Musgrove
Holliday	McGehee	Nelson
Holt	McGehee & Daniel	Noble
Hubbard	McGlasson	Nunnally
Hudson	McHudson	Nunnelly
Hughes	McNutt	Nunnerly
Hunt	Meador	Osborn
Hurt	Meadore	Osborne
Jackson	Meadow	Overby
James	Medley	Overton
J'Anson	Metteaner	Owen
Jeffress	Michaux	Paulett
Jenkins	Mickle	Pearson
Johns	Middleton	Penick
Johnson	Miller	Perkinson
Jones	Mills	Perrin
Knight	Mohorn	Peters
Lacy	Mohorus	Pettus
Lambert	Moore	Phillips
Leffew	Morehorn	Pigg
Leigh	Morgan	Porter
Leneve	Moring	Price
Ligon	Morrison	Priddy

Virginia Slave Births Index, 1853-1865, Geographic Supplement

Prince Edward	Prince Edward	Prince Edward
Raine	Taylor	White
Read	Terry	Whitehead
Redd	Thackston	Whiteman
Redford	Thompson	Wilkerson
Rice	Thornton	Williams
Richardson	Thweatt	Williamson
Riggins	Todd	Wilson
Ritchie	Treadway	Wiltse
Robertson	Tredway	Witt
Rodgers	Trueheart	Womack
Routon	Tucker	Wood
Rowlett	Tuggle	Woodall
Rowton	Tuggles	Woodson
Rudd	Vaughan	Wooton
Sampson	Venable	Wootten
Sanders	Waddill	Wootton
Scott	Wade	Worsham
Shackleton	Walker	Wright
Shepherd	Wall	Yarbrough
Simmons	Walton	Young
Smith	Watkins	**Prince Edward/Nottoway**
Smithson	Watson	Foster
Snead	Weaver	**Prince Edward/Richmond**
Sneed	Webb	Anderson
Spencer	Wells	**Prince George**
Sterne	West	Adams
Stewart	Wharey	Aiken
Stokes	Whary	Akin
Stuart	Wheary	Akins
Taliaferro	Wheeler	Aldridge

Prince George	Prince George	Prince George
Alley	Brodnax	Figg
America	Brownley	Finn
Avery	Brownly	Finny
Baird	Bryant	Friend
Barrow	Burrow	Fuqua
Batte	Butts	Gary
Baxter	Cain	Gatling
Baylie	Caine	Gee
Baylor	Calquehoun	Gennett
Beasley	Chappell	George
Beesley	Clarke	Gilliam
Beesly	Cock	Girlbey
Belcher	Cocke	Gordan
Bell	Cole	Grammer
Belsher	Collier	Grasswitt
Birchett	Combis	Gray
Birdsong	Comer	Gregory
Bland	Cumbie	Griffith
Blankenship	Daniel	Gurley
Bolling	Daniels	Haddon
Bonner	Dunn	Hair
Bott	Dupuy	Hall
Botte	Eldridge	Hare
Bowden	Epes	Harris
Bowling	Eppes	Harrison
Bowry	Epps	Harwell
Bragg	Evans	Hatch
Briggs	Fenn	Hawkins
Broadnax	Fenner	Heath
Brockwell	Fewqua	Hill

Virginia Slave Births Index, 1853-1865, Geographic Supplement

Prince George	Prince George	Prince George
Hite	Organ	Simpson
Hobbs	Osborne	Smith
Hollingsworth	Osburn	Southall
Hurt	Parham	Spain
Jennings	Parsons	Spiers
Jones	Peebes	Spratley
Jordan	Peebles	Sprigg
Judkins	Peterson	Stainback
King	Petway	Stracham
Knox	Phillips	Stricker
Land	Pleasants	Sturdivant
Leath	Proctor	Tatum
Lee	Raines	Taylor
Leonard	Rainey	Temple
Lilly	Raney	Thweatt
Livesay	Rives	Tilly
Livesy	Roane	Tucker
Lucado	Rowland	Velin
Lucadoe	Rowlett	Vellines
Lucadoo	Rudder	Walsh
Magee	Ruffin	Walthal
Marks	Rushmore	Warren
Mason	Russell	Warthal
McCann	Scarborough	Warthall
McGee	Scott	Warthen
McHann	Shackleford	Webb
Moody	Shand	Weiseger
Moore	Shands	Wells
Newcomb	Sheffield	Whitmore
Orgain	Simmons	Wilcox

Virginia Slave Births Index, 1853-1865, Geographic Supplement

Prince George	Prince William	Prince William
Wilkins	Burgess	Foley
Willcox	Butler	Folson
Williams	Cannon	Foote
Williamson	Carter	Foster
Wills	Chancellor	Fuller
Winfree	Chapman	Gaines
Wiseman	Chinn	Gale
Wood	Clark	Gibson
Young	Clarke	Glasscock
Prince George/Dinwiddie	Cockrell	Godfrey
Butts	Compton	Graham
Spiers	Conrad	Gray
Tucker	Conrod	Grayson
Prince George/Norfolk	Corson	Green
Cole	Cushing	Groves
Prince George/Petersburg	Dade	Haisley
Cole	Davis	Haislip
Prince William	Dogan	Hamilton
Atkinson	Douglass	Hancock
Bailey	Dulany	Hancock (Est)
Balch	Duvall	Harrison
Ball	Edmonds	Heath
Barbee	Edmonis	Hickerson
Bayly	Ellis	Hite
Beedle	Evans	Hixson
Bell	Ewell	Holmes
Berkeley	Fewell	Hooe
Berkley	Fitzgerald	Hord
Brawner	Fitzhugh	House
Brooks	Florance	Howison

Virginia Slave Births Index, 1853-1865, Geographic Supplement

Prince William	Prince William	Prince William
Hunton	Norville	Windser
Hutchinson	Nutt	Wright
Hutchison	Purcell	Wroe
Jennings	Roach	**Prince William/Fairfax**
Johnson	Robinson	Hooe
Jones	Roe	**Prince William/Fauquier**
Kincheloe	Selecman	Morgan
Latham	Shirley	Nutt
Latimer	Simpson	**Prince William/Pittsylvania**
Leachman	Sinclair	Carter
Lee	Smith	**Prince William/Stafford**
Lewis	Stewart	Tolson
Lipscomb	Stonnell	**Princess Anne**
Lynn	Stonnill	Ackies
Macrae	Stuart	Atwood
Maddox	Taylor	Baker
Marders	Thornton	Banks
Marsteller	Thurman	Barnes
McCoy	Tolson	Baum
McIntosh	Towles	Baxter
McLean	Turner	Bell
McMullen	Tyler	Benthall
McPherson	Vermillion	Bonney
Meade	Walker	Bonny
Merchant	Washington	Bowen
Mount	Weedon	Bradford
Muschett	Weir	Braithwait
Mushett	Wigginton	Braithwaite
Nelson	Willcoxon	Brewer
Newman	Williams	Bright

Virginia Slave Births Index, 1853-1865, Geographic Supplement

Princess Anne	Princess Anne	Princess Anne
Brock	Fentress	Joice
Brockett	Ferebee	Jones
Brown	Fisher	Keeling
Burgess	Flanagan	Kellum
Burroughs	Flemming	Lambert
Butt	Foreman	Land
Caffee	Foster	Lee
Caffey	Garrison	Lewis
Campbell	Godfrey	Macon
Cannon	Gornto	Malbone
Capps	Gornts	Mallory
Cason	Gregory	McAlpine
Chaplain	Gresham Est	McClanan
Corbell	Griggs	McIntosh
Cornick	Grimstead	McKemmy
Cox	Hartley	Miller
Davis	Haynes	Moore
Dawley	Henley	Morgan
Doudge	Herbert	Morris
Dozier	Hill	Morrisett
Dudley	Hoggard	Munden
Dyer	Holstead	Murden
Eaton	Hubbard	Murray
Edmonds	Hunter	Nicholson
Edmonis	Hutchings	Nimmo
Edwards	Ingram	Old
Elwell	Ives	Overstreet
Etheredge	Jacobs	Paynter
Etheridge	James	Peters
Ewell	Johnson	Petty

Virginia Slave Births Index, 1853-1865, Geographic Supplement

Princess Anne	Princess Anne	Pulaski
Philips	Williamson	Currin
Rainey	Wilson	Darst
Randolph	Wise	Doobins
Roberts	Wolse	Draper
Rogers	Woodard	Eaton
Salmons	Woodhouse	Ewing
Scott	Wright	Glendy
Seneca	**Pulaski**	Graham
Sheppard	Aiken	Grantham
Shield	Alexander	Grayson
Sikes	Allison	Guthrie
Simmons	Bell	Hedge
Smith	Bentley	Hoge
Sparrow	Bently	Honaker
Stone	Bill	Howe
Styron	Boyce	Hudson
Tatem	Boyd	Hunter
Temple	Breeding	Ingram
Thompson	Brown	Jordan
Thomson	Bullard	Kent
Thorowgood	Caffee	King
Twiford	Calfee	Lloyd
Vaughan	Cecil	Martin
Walke	Chumbley	Mastin
Ward	Chumney	Mathews
Warden	Cloyd	McGavock
Waterfield	Coffee	Miller
West	Criner	Morehead
Whitehurst	Crockett	Morgan
Williams	Currier	Muirhead

Virginia Slave Births Index, 1853-1865, Geographic Supplement

Pulaski	Pulaski/Montgomery	Rappahannock
O'Dell	Mathews	Butler
Owens	**Pulaski/Powhatan**	Bywaters
Peirce	Miller	Camp
Pierce	**Rappahannock**	Campbell
Poage	Alsop	Cannon
Rains	Amiss	Cargill
Sayers	Anderson	Carpenter
Shearman	Atkins	Carver
Shepherd	Baggarly	Chanceller
Shurman	Baker	Chancellor
Sloan	Ball	Chappelear
Slone	Barbee	Cheek
Stone	Beggarly	Chelf
Summers	Bell	Coffage
Taylor	Berry	Colbert
Tinkle	Blackwell	Compton
Trinkle	Botts	Cooksey
Trolinger	Bowerset	Coppage
Trollinger	Bowersett	Corbin
Vermillion	Brady	Corder
Vickers	Bragg	Corley
Watson	Branson	Cowgill
Wilson	Brook	Creel
Wood	Brown	Cropp
Woolwine	Browning	Daniel
Wygal	Browning & Smith	Darden
Wysor	Buckner	Daris
Pulaski/Giles	Bundy	Davis
Hoge	Burgess	Dean
	Burke	Dear

Virginia Slave Births Index, 1853-1865, Geographic Supplement

Rappahannock	Rappahannock	Rappahannock
Dearing	Harres	Leavell
Deatherage	Harris	Lillard
Demmings	Harriss	Lillars
Dennis	Heterick	Major
Detherage	Hisle	Martin
Dowden	Hitt	Mason
Dudley	Holland	Massie
Duncan	Holmes	McQueen
Eastham	Hood	Menefee
Field	Hopkins	Menifee
Fisher	Hudson	Millan
Fletcher	Huff	Miller
Fogg	Huffman	Moffett
Fosset	Hughes	Moore
Fossett	Hume	Mosingo
Freeman	Jackson	Murphy
Fristoe	Jasper	Nelson
Grant	Jeffress	Newby
Green	Jeffries	O'Bannon
Griffin	Jett	O'Banon
Grigsby	Johnson	Palmer
Grimsley	Jones	Parks
Groves	Jordan	Partlow
Hackley	Kelly	Payne
Haddox	Kemper	Peyton
Hambric	Kinsey	Pierce
Hambrick	Lane	Popham
Hand	Late	Powers
Hanres	Latham	Priest
Harner	Latouradais	Ramey

Virginia Slave Births Index, 1853-1865, Geographic Supplement

Rappahannock	Rappahannock	Rappahannock/Washington
Ramy	Spindle	Kinsey
Rawles	Stark	**Richmond City**
Reager	Starke	Adams
Reamy	Stone	Allen
Reed	Surley	Alvis
Reid	Swindler	Ambler
Ricketts	Tapp	Anderson
Roads	Thornhill	Apperson
Roberson	Thornton	Archer
Roberts	Thorp	Armistead
Rollins	Thurston	Armstrong
Romine	Turley	Bagby
Rouzie	Turner	Bailey
Rowzie	Updike	Baker
Rudasile	Utterback	Ballard
Rudasill	Voss	Bargamin
Rudasilla	Walden	Barham
Rudasille	Walter	Baum
Sanders	Waters	Beale
Saunders	Welch	Bentley
Scott	White	Blair
Sears	Whitescarver	Bolling
Settle	Willis	Bosher
Singleton	Wilson	Boulware
Skinner	Wood	Bowen
Slaughter	Woodard	Bowery
Sloane	Woodward	Bowles
Smith	Yancey	Bradley
Smith & Browing	Yancy	Bransford
Smith & Browning	Yates	Brock

Virginia Slave Births Index, 1853-1865, Geographic Supplement

Richmond City	Richmond City	Richmond City
Brook	Cross	Fleishman
Brooks	Crump	Flernoy
Brown	Crutchfield	Fletcher
Burch	Dabney	Ford
Burton	Dade	Foster
Butler	Dandridge	Fox
Cabell	Darracott	Franklin
Camp	Davis	Frayser
Campbell	Dean	Gamble
Carter	Deaton	Garnett
Carver	Delcampo	Garrett
Chenery	Denoon	Gary
Cherallia	Denton	Gilliam
Childrey	Dewitt	Glazebrook
Chiles	Dickinson	Glenn
Claiborne	Dill	Goddin
Clarke	Dimmock	Graham
Clemmitt	Dodamead	Grant
Cobbs	Donnan	Gray
Cohen	Dormin	Greanor
Coleman	Dudley	Green
Collin	Dunford	Greenhow
Conway	Dunton	Gregory
Cook	Ellett	Gretter
Cook & Toler	Elliott	Griffin
Cottrell	Ellis	Griwold
Cough	Elmore	Grubbs
Crenshaw	Enders	Gwathmey
Crew	England	Hagan
Cringen	Ferguson	Hall

Virginia Slave Births Index, 1853-1865, Geographic Supplement

Richmond City	Richmond City	Richmond City
Hancock	Ladd	Meredith
Hardgrove	Langhorne	Merriwether
Hargrove	Lankford	Miller
Harrison	Lawson	Minnigerode
Harwood	Lee	Minor
Haxall	Lester	Moore
Heath	Levy	Morgan
Hill	Lewellen	Morris
Hobson	Libby	Morriss
Hoelfich	Ligon	Morsen & Sedden
Holeman	Linton	Morson
Holman	Lipscomb	Morton
Hook	Lockett	Mosby
Horner	Lumpkin	Murray
Howard	Lumpkins	Myers
Howell	Lynch	Neoin
Hundley	Macan	Newburn
Hunt	Macon	Norton
Hunter	Martin	Nott
Jackson	Mayo	Nuckols
Jacob	Mays	Olphin
James	McCance	Omohundro
Jeter	McCann	Palmer
Johnson	McCardy	Parker
Johnston	McCarthy	Patty
Jones	McCaw	Payne
Keesee	McFarland	Pearce
Kennon	McGee	Pemberton
Kent	McGruder	Pendleton
King	Meade	Philips

Virginia Slave Births Index, 1853-1865, Geographic Supplement

Richmond City	Richmond City	Richmond City
Pleasants	Sinton	Temple
Pollard	Sizer	Thomas
Porter	Skipwith	Thornton
Potly	Slater	Tighe
Powell	Sledd	Timberlake
Priddy	Smith	Tinsley
Punton	Sneed	Todd
Quarles	Solomon	Toler & Cook
Ragland	Stagg	Totty
Randolph	Stairs	Trent
Rawlings	Stanard	Trice
Redd	Starke	Tucker
Redwood	Sterling	Tunley
Robinson	Stewart	Turnley
Rosenbaum	Stokes	Tyler
Row	Stone	Valentine
Rowe	Stratton	Vaugh
Royester	Sublett	Vyse
Ruslow	Sutherland	Waddell
Sands	Sutten	Wade
Saunders	Sweeney	Walden
Scammell	Sydnor	Walker
Scott	Tabb	Wallace
Seabrook	Talbott	Waller
Sedwick	Taliaferro	Walthall
Selden	Talley	Warwick
Shelton	Tanner	Watkins
Sheppard	Tardy	Watson
Short	Tate	Watt
Sidnor	Taylor	Wayt

Virginia Slave Births Index, 1853-1865, Geographic Supplement

Richmond City	Richmond Co	Richmond Co
Wayte	Biscoe	Dewbry
Weisiger	Booker	Dickenson
Wharton	Bowser	Dickerson
White	Bramham	Dishman
Whiting	Braxton	Dobyns
Whitlock	Brockenborough	Dudley
Wilkinson	Brockenborugh	Dunaway
Williams	Brockenbrough	English
Wilson	Brokenbrough	Fauntleroy
Winston	Broocks	Ficklin
Womble	Brooke	Fleet
Wood	Brown	Garland
Wooldridge	Bryant	Gooch
Word	Burnard	Gordan
Wortham	Callahan	Gray
Wyatt	Carter	Gresham
Wynne	Carther	Hale
Yale	Chines	Hall
Richmond City/Albemarle	Chinn	Hanson
Montiero	Clark	Harding
Richmond Co	Clarke	Hardwick
Alderson	Coleman	Harris
Baird	Connelly	Harwood
Balderson	Connolly	Haynes
Ball	Crabb	Hayth
Barton	Cralle	Hazzard
Baynham	Critcher	Headley
Belfield	Curtis	Henry
Bell	Cutchin	Hipkins
Bernard	Davenport	Howard

Virginia Slave Births Index, 1853-1865, Geographic Supplement

Richmond Co	Richmond Co	Richmond Co
Hutt	Payne	Thrifts
Ingram	Pear	Walker
Jeffries	Pearson	Wallace
Johnson	Phillips	Webb
Jones	Pitts	Wellford
Lamkin	Pitzer	Willford
Landon	Pleasants	Wood
Latham	Porter	Woolard
Lemoine	Pridham	Wright
Little	Pritchett	Yeatman
Luttrell	Rainers	Yerby
Lyell	Rains	**Roanoke**
McCarty	Rice	Campbell
McClanahan	Rich	Chapman
Middleton	Richardson	Clanahan
Mitchell	Rockwell	Hartley
Montgomery	Sanders	Harvey
Morris	Sandy	James
Morriss	Saunders	Johnston
Mothershead	Scott	Miller
Motley	Self	Oliver
Neale	Settle	Turner
Northen	Shackleford	**Roanoke Co**
Northern	Smith	Alcorn
Oldham	Spence	Alexander
Omohundro	Tallent	Asbury
Owen	Tayloe	Balthis
Owens	Taylor	Bandy
Pare	Tebbs	Barnett
Parry	Thompson	Bass

Virginia Slave Births Index, 1853-1865, Geographic Supplement

Roanoke Co	Roanoke Co	Roanoke Co
Betts	Duckwiler	Jackson
Board	Eddington	Johnston
Bon	Edington	Keiser
Bondurant	Evans	Kent
Bonsack	Fears	Kyle
Boon	Fleming	Langhorn
Bouldin	Forsythe	Langhorne
Brand	Fowler	Lewis
Brilhart	Franklin	Lumford
Brill	Frantz	Lunsford
Brown	Furrow	McChesney
Brugh	Garst	McClanahan
Burk	Gish	McCorkle
Burks	Gleeson	McGeorge
Burwell	Goodwin	Miller
Bush	Griffin	Montague
Bushong	Hannah	Murray
Campbell	Hansborough	Murrey
Carvin	Hansbrough	Muse
Chapman	Harding	Myers
Cole	Harvey	Neal
Conkle	Hatcher	Neff
Cooper	Hawley	Oliver
Crawford	Hersh	Patterson
Dabney	Hershberger	Persinger
Davis	Holt	Pettie
Deaton	Howley	Pettijohn
Dennis	Huff	Pettit
Deyerle	Hupp	Petty
Diuguid	Hurt	Peyton

Virginia Slave Births Index, 1853-1865, Geographic Supplement

Roanoke Co	Roanoke Co	Rockbridge
Philips	Thomas	Adams
Phillips	Thrasher	Alexander
Pitzer	Tinsley	Alphin
Power	Trent	Amole
Powers	Trout	Armentrout
Preston	Utz	Armintrout
Price	Vinyard	Arnold
Read	Walton	Bachtel
Reed	Watt	Bachtell
Ribble	Watts	Bacon
Richardson	Wells	Baker
Rives	White	Baldwin
Robertson	Williams	Barclay
Robinson	Williamson	Barton
Rorer	Winkler	Baxter
Rout	Wood	Beard
Routt	Woods	Bell
Ruddell	Wright	Benton
Saunders	Yates	Bowyer
Shanks	Zirkle	Bradford
Simmons	**Roanoke Co/Albemarle**	Bradley
Smith	Brown	Brafford
Snider	**Roanoke Co/WV**	Braford
Snyder	Betts	Brockenbrough
Spessard	**Rockbridge**	Brown
Taylor	Abraham	Buchanan
Terrell	Ackerby	Buckner
Terrill	Ackerley	Burk
Terry	Ackerly	Burke
Thaxton	Adair	Burks

Rockbridge	Rockbridge	Rockbridge
Cameron	Edmundson	Hodge
Campbell	Edward	Holden
Carson	Effinger	Hopkins
Chandler	Elhart	Houston
Chapin	Ewing	Howard
Clarkson	Firbaugh	Huff
Coffman	Frazier & Randolph	Hutcheson
Colston	Fuller	Hutchison
Compton	Garland	Hyde
Conner	Gibson	Jefferson & Pendleton
Cox	Gilmore	Jerry
Craig	Glasgow	Johns
Crawford	Gold	Johnson
Culton	Goodloe	Johnston
Cumings	Goodman	Jones
Cumming	Goodwin	Jordan
Cummings	Goyne	Jordon
Cummins	Graham	Junkin
Curry	Greenlee	Kennedy
Davidson	Grigsby	Kerr
Davis	Gurley	Kiger
Dixon	Hamilton	Kinnear
Dold	Harper	Kirkpatrick
Donald	Harris	Kyger
Douglass	Hartsock	Lackey
Dryden	Hartsook	Laird
Eades	Hatcher	Larell
Eads	Henderson	Larew
Echart	Hepler	Lavell
Edmondson	Hileman	Leckey

Virginia Slave Births Index, 1853-1865, Geographic Supplement

Rockbridge	Rockbridge	Rockbridge
Leech	McCutchan	Pitman
Lewis	McDanald	Poague
Leyburn	McDaniel	Poindexter
Lincoln	McDowell	Pultz
Lindsay	McElwes	Rader
Link	McFaddin	Randolph & Frazier
Locher	McHenry	Ranson
Locker	McKee	Reace
Logan	McKenny	Reid
Lowman	McKinsey	Richeson
Lusk	McNutt	Rogers
Luster	McWilson	Ruff
Lyle	Michie	Sale
Mackey	Miller	Salling
Major	Moffett	Sanders
Mann	Mohler	Sandford
Mason	Montgomery	Shafer
Massie	Moore	Shaffer
Mateer	Morrison	Shaver
Matheny	Morton	Sheltman
McBride	Mosely	Shepherdson
McCaul	Myers	Shields
McChesney	O'Dell	Short
McClintic	Paine	Shorter
McCluer	Parry	Sloane
McClung	Patterson	Smith
McCorkle	Paxton	Spotsylvania
McCormick	Pendleton	Steele
McCown	Pendleton & Jefferson	Stephen
McCray	Pettigrew	Sterrett

Virginia Slave Births Index, 1853-1865, Geographic Supplement

Rockbridge	Rockbridge	Rockingham
Stevens	Witt	Catlett
Stoner	Wright	Chrisman
Strain	Youel	Coffman
Straine	Zollman	Cole
Stuart	Zollmann	Conrad
Taylor	**Rockingham**	Cook
Templeton	Alder	Cootes
Thompson	Allen	Cowan
Trevey	Ammon	Cowen
Trice	Argabright	Crawford
Trimble	Banger	Cromer
Trotter	Barger	Davidson
Turpin	Barley	Davis
Tutwiler	Baugher	Davison
Walker	Beal	Deneale
Wallace	Bear	Dever
Watson	Beard	Devier
Watts	Blackford	Dice
Weaver	Blain	Dinkel
Webb	Boon	Dinkle
Weir	Bowman	Dove
White	Branner	Dovel
Whitmore	Brenner	Dundore
Wiley	Brock	Dunevant
Williamson	Brown	Eastham
Willson	Burgess	Effinger
Wilmore	Burner	Eiler
Wilson	Byerly	Elliott
Winn	Campbell	Ervine
Withrow	Carpenter	Erwin

Virginia Slave Births Index, 1853-1865, Geographic Supplement

Rockingham	Rockingham	Rockingham
Evans	Henton	Maupin
Ewin	Herring	Mauzy
Flook	Hill	McKyle
Fox	Homan	Miller
Fulton	Hoover	Moffett
Funkhouser	Hopkins	Moore
Gaines	Hornsberger	Morris
Gambell	Irvine	Newman
Gambill	Keezil	Ott
Gibbons	Kemper	Palmer
Gilmore	Kenney	Peal
Gochenour	Keran	Pennybacker
Gordan	Keyser	Pennybecker
Gordon	Kirtley	Perry
Gray	Kisling	Peyton
Grim	Kite	Rhodes
Gullihugh	Koogler	Riley
Haines	Koontz	Ritenour
Hainsber	Kurtley	Robinson
Hansberger	Kyle	Rodgers
Hardesty	Layton	Roller
Harmon	Lee	Ruffner
Harnsbarger	Lewis	Rust
Harnsberger	Lincoln	Seay
Harris	Lindsey	Sellers
Harrison	Loffland	Shacklett
Haynes	Lofland	Shafer
Hedrick	Long	Shank
Hendrick	Martz	Shaver
Henebarger	Mauck	Shoap

Virginia Slave Births Index, 1853-1865, Geographic Supplement

Rockingham	Rockingham	Russell
Sigler	Zirkle	Gibson
Sites	**Russell**	Gillespie
Smith	Alderson	Gilmen
Snider	Alexander	Gint
Spears	Banner	Gray
Speck	Baylor	Hackney
Spindle	Bickley	Hanson
Stephens	Boyd	Hargis
Strawther	Browing	Harton
Strayer	Browning	Hawkins
Thompson	Burdine	Hendricks
Thurmond	Campbell	Horn
Wanger	Carrell	Howard
Warren	Carter	Jesse
Wartman	Combs	Jessee
Weaver	Cummings	Johnson
West	Dickenson	Kiser
Williams	Dickerson	Lampkin
Williamson	Dickinson	Lee
Wingfield	Dorton	Litten
Wise	Ferguson	Litton
Wolf	Ferrell	Luce
Wynant	Fletcher	Mullins
Yancey	Frick	Muncy
Yancy	Fugate	Nash
Yoste	Fullen	Osborn
Yount	Furguson	Osborne
Zegler	Gardner	Pruner
Zerkel	Garrett	Riley
Zirkel	Gent	Samples

Virginia Slave Births Index, 1853-1865, Geographic Supplement

Russell	Scott	Shenandoah
Smith	Jett	Allen
Sykes	Johnson	Arts
Thomas	Johnston	Beal
Tignor	Jones	Billings
Vermillion	Kane	Borden
Webb	Kilgore	Bowman
Scott	Lane	Bragg
Anderson	Lee	Branner
Balentine	Lyon	Burner
Bickley	Mann	Bushong
Boatright	Mason	Clem
Browning	Mayabb	Dinges
Byrd	Mayson	Douglass
Compton	McConnell	Dulaney
Cox	McKenzee	Feriby
Deckerson	McKinney	Fox
Dickinson	McKinsey	Fry
Dorton	Minter	Gatewood
Dulaney	Morison	Haas
Dykes	Morrison	Hamman
Epperson	Petyjohn	Hammon
Ewing	Ramsey	Headley
Fulkerson	Salling	Hoshour
Garnett	Shoemaker	Hupp
Gillenwaters	Smith	Hushour
Godsey	Speer	Jackson
Haynes	Strong	Kendrick
Herron	Vienyard	Koontz
Hilton	Wolfe	Lantz
Horton	Wood	Lee

Virginia Slave Births Index, 1853-1865, Geographic Supplement

Shenandoah	Smyth	Smyth
Meem	Ashland	Kincannon
Miller	Ashlen	Kirk
Moore	Ashley	Lansdown
Newell	Atkins	Leonard
Newman	Beatie	McCarty
Nowell	Blankenbaker	Morgan
Ott	Bonham	Musser
Pennywit	Brown	Nelson
Pifer	Buchanan	Painter
Pitman	Byar	Pearson
Prichard	Campbell	Person
Quick	Cole	Porter
Rice	Copenhaver	Porterfield
Richardson	Cox	Poston
Rinker	Davis	Preston
Rudolph	Dutton	Roberts
Rush	Fowler	Robertson
Satterwhite	Fulton	Saint John
Shirley	Goolsby	Sanders
Sibert	Grayson	Scott
Sigler	Greever	Sexton
Strayer	Groseclose	Shugart
Thompson	Hamilton	Sipes
Trout	Harris	Snavely
Walton	Hays	Spinkle
Wander	Horn	Spratt
Zirkle	Hubble	Sprinkle
Smyth	James	Stakes
Aker	Johnston	Strother
Annaway	Jones	Talbert

Smyth	Southampton	Southampton
Tate	Benton	Darden
Tate & Bros	Blow	Daughtrey
Taylor	Boykin	Davis
Thomas	Branch	Denegra
Thompson	Briggs	Denigre
Thumon	Brister	Devany
Thurmon	Bristor	Dillard
Tilson	Britt	Doles
Townsend	Brittle	Drew
Umbarger	Bryant	Drewry
Vance	Burges	Drury
Ward	Burgess	Duck
Watson	Butler	Dunn
Williams	Butt	Edwards
Wolfe	Butts	Ellis
Southampton	Cable	Eppes
Adams	Camp	Epps
Applewhite	Carnes	Everett
Arnold	Carr	Fires
Atkins	Charles	Fitch
Atkinson	Claud	Frances
Bailey	Clayton	Francis
Barham	Clements	Gardner
Barker	Cobb	Gay
Barnes	Cook	Gillett
Barrett	Cornwell	Gillette
Beale	Councill	Gilliam
Beaton	Cross	Gilliam (Est)
Bell	Crump	Goodwin
Bendall	Crumpler	Goodwyn

Virginia Slave Births Index, 1853-1865, Geographic Supplement

Southampton	Southampton	Southampton
Gray	Joyner	Newsom
Griffin	Judkins	Nicholson
Grizzard	Kello	Nives
Gurley	Kindred	Norfleet
Hall	Kitchen	Oberry
Harcum	Langford	Parker
Hargrave	Lankford	Person
Harris	Lawrence	Persons
Hart	Leigh	Peters
Harvell	Liner	Pettway
Henderson	Linor	Pond
Hill	Linow	Pope
Hines	Little	Popes & Murfee
Holland	Maget	Porter
Holleman	Magett	Powell
Holmes	Magette	Prestlow
Holt	Majett	Pretlow
Hood	Majette	Prince
Hope	Mason	Raiford
Howell	Massenburg	Rawling
Hundley	McClenny	Rawlings
Hurt	McMiala	Rawls
Ivey	Miller	Reese
Ivy	Moore	Ricks
James	Murfee & Popes	Ridley
Janagam	Murrell	Rollings
Jenkins	Musgrave	Rollins
Johnson	Myrick	Rowe
Jones	Neal	Rowland
Jordan	Neale	Ruse

Virginia Slave Births Index, 1853-1865, Geographic Supplement

Southampton	Southampton	Spotsylvania
Ryland	Whitney	Boulevard
Scarborough	Wiggins	Boulware
Scott	Williams	Bowen
Screws	Williamson	Boxley
Sebrell	Worrell	Brent
Simmons	Wyrick	Brightwell
Sledge	**Southampton/Brunswick**	Brock
Smith	Blunt	Brook
Spivy	**Southampton/Isle of Wight**	Brooke
Stephens	Cross	Brooks
Stephenson	**Southampton/NC**	Brown
Stith	Majett	Browne
Story	**Spotsylvania**	Buckner
Summerall	Abbott	Bullard
Summervell	Alsop	Bullock
Sykes	Anderson	Burruss
Thomas	Andrew	Butler
Thorp	Andrews	Cammack
Turner	Arnold	Canohan
Urquart	Ball	Carner
Urquhart	Ballard	Carnes
Vaughan	Baptist	Carpenter
Vick	Beazley	Carter
Waller	Bell	Cason
Warren	Beverley	Chancellor
Webb	Beverly	Chandler
Wells	Billingsley	Charlters
Westbrook	Blaydes	Chewning
White	Bledsoe	Coates
Whitehead	Boggs	Colbert

Virginia Slave Births Index, 1853-1865, Geographic Supplement

Spotsylvania	Spotsylvania	Spotsylvania
Coleman	Duvall	Hambleton
Collins	Edenton	Hamilton
Connor	Edinton	Hancock
Cor	Elley	Hansbrough
Cox	Estes	Harris
Crawford	Farish	Harrison
Crismond	Faulconer	Harrow
Cropp	Fife	Hart
Crutchfield	Flippo	Haslop
Dabney	Ford	Hatcher
Dardall	Foster	Haydon
Davis	Fourneyhough	Heislop
Day	Frazer	Henshaw
Decker	Frazier	Herndon
DeJarnett	Furneyhough	Herring
DeJarnette	Gardner	Heslep
Dicken	Garland	Hicks
Dickenson	Garnett	Hildrup
Dickinson	Gatewood	Hill
Dillard	Gayle	Hockaday
Dismeux	Gerrell	Hodges
Dismukes	Gibson	Holladay
Dobyns	Goodloe	Horn
Doggett	Goodwin	Houser
Dowdall	Gordon	Houseworth
Downer	Grady	Howerson
Dudley	Graves	Humphries
Duerson	Green	Iseman
Duke	Hailey	Jenkins
Durrett	Hall	Jerrell

Virginia Slave Births Index, 1853-1865, Geographic Supplement

Spotsylvania	Spotsylvania	Spotsylvania
Johnson	Patton	Schooler
Jones	Payne	Scott
Kendall	Peake	Seay
Kesler	Pendleton	Shackelford
Kube	Pettus	Shackleford
Lacy	Peyton	Simms
Landram	Phillips	Smith
Landrum	Pierce	Spindle
Lee	Pool	Staiar
Levy	Powell	Stanard
Lewis	Pratt	Stansberry
Lipscomb	Pritchett	Stansbury
Long	Proctor	Stephens
Luck	Pulliam	Stewart
Martin	Quarles	Straughan
Mason	Quisenberry	Stubbs
Massey	Rawling	Talley
Mastin	Rawlings	Taylor
McCalley	Rennolds	Temple
McCally	Richards	Thacker
McCloud	Richardson	Timberlake
McCracken	Richerson	Tinder
McDonald	Richeson	Tompkins
McGhee	Robinson	Towles
McKenney	Row	Trigg
McKinney	Rowe	Turnley
Minor	Sale	Twyman
Nuckols	Samuel	Tyler
Parker	Sanford	Vass
Partlow	Sarrell	Waller

Virginia Slave Births Index, 1853-1865, Geographic Supplement

Spotsylvania	Stafford	Stafford
Walters	Bloxton	Edwards
Webber	Botts	Eustece
Wharton	Bray	Fitzhugh
Wheller	Bridges	Flatford
Whisler	Bridwell	Forbes
White	Briggs	Ford
Whitton	Brooke	Franklin
Wiatt	Browne	French
Wiglesworth	Buckannan	Fritter
Willoughby	Burton	Froble
Wilson	Carter	George
Winn	Catlet	Goodrick
Wright	Chinn	Gordon
Yerby	Clark	Gray
Young	Clift	Greaves
Spotsylvania/Caroline	Coakley	Green
Burruss	Coalter	Hansberger
Stafford	Combs	Harding
Adie	Conway	Harris
Alexander	Conyers	Harrison
Alsop	Cooke	Hay
Anthony	Corbin	Hedgeman
Ashby	Crone	Hedgman
Ball	Cropp	Henry
Ballard	Curtis	Herndon
Barber	Daffan	Hewett
Barnes	Daniel	Hickerson
Bell	Davis	Holms
Benson	Dunbar	Hooe
Blake	Edington	Hore

Virginia Slave Births Index, 1853-1865, Geographic Supplement

Stafford	Stafford	Stafford
Hull	Norman	Stern
Humphrey	O'Bannon	Sterne
Humphries	Payne	Stevens
James	Perry	Stewart
Jameson	Peterson	Sthreshley
Jones	Petty	Stone
Keith	Pollard	Streshley
Kellogg	Pollock	Strother
Kendall	Powers	Sullivan
King	Prichard	Suttle
Knight	Ramey	Swetnam
Lacy	Ramy	Tacket
Latham	Riley	Tackett
Lee	Rose	Taliaferro
Lowry	Rowe	Taylor
Lucas	Sanford	Thompson
Lunsford	Schooler	Timberlake
Mason	Scott	Tolson
Masters	Scott & Minor	Towson
Matthews	Sedden	Wallace
McCoy	Seddon	Waller
Meredith	Shackleford	Wallis
Minor	Shelket	Wamsley
Minor & Scott	Shelton	Warren
Moncure	Skinker	Weaver
Moore	Smith	Williams
Morgan	Spindle	Withers
Morson	Stark	**Staunton**
Morton	Starke	Bledsoe
Nelson	Stephens	Castleman

Virginia Slave Births Index, 1853-1865, Geographic Supplement

Staunton	Surry	Surry
Covell	Baugh	Epps
Crawford	Bell	Faison
Donaghe	Berryman	Faulcon
Edmondson	Bishop	Finch
Eskridge	Boling	Fitchett
Fultz	Booth	Flowers
Gray	Brown	Gill
Hall	Burt	Goodrich
Harman	Carter	Grant
Imboden	Charles	Graves
Kayser	Clark	Gwaltney
Lushbaugh	Clarke	Hall
McCue	Clary	Hankins
Merillat	Clayton	Harris
Peck	Clements	Hart
Peyton	Cofer	Hawkins
Phillips	Cole	Hines
Points	Collier	Holleman
Stribling	Crenshaw	Holloway
Thompson	Crump	Holt
Warden	Davis	Hood
Wayt	Deal	Jones
Surry	Delk	Judkins
Adams	Dew	King
Andrews	Dillard	Lamb
Atkinson	Drew	Land
Bage	Edward	Lane
Bailey	Edwards	Maddera
Baird	Ellis	Mason
Barham	Emmery	Maynard

Virginia Slave Births Index, 1853-1865, Geographic Supplement

Surry	Sussex	Sussex
McAllister	Adkin	Butts
Morris	Adkins	Capell
Murdaugh	Aldridge	Cassell
Nellums	Andrews	Chamberliss
Parsons	Atkinson	Chambliss
Pond	Bailey	Champion
Pretlow	Bain	Chapell
Rainey	Baine	Chappel
Roberts	Baird	Chappell
Rowell	Barham	Clarke
Ruffin	Barker	Clary
Savedge	Barrett	Clements
Selden	Basdam	Cobb
Simpson	Bass	Cocks
Sledge	Baugh	Cogbill
Smith	Belches	Collier
Spratley	Belsches	Cotton
Stewart	Belsches & Dunn	Creath
Sykes	Bendall	Cross
Tatum	Birdsong	Davis
Taylor	Bishop	Dearing
Warren	Blow	Dillard
Watkins	Blowe	Dobie
West	Blunt	Downman
White	Booth	Drewry
Williamson	Bowden	Drumright
Wilson	Briggs	Drumwright
Wrenn	Broadbent	Dunn
Sussex	Brown	Dunn & Belsches
Adams	Burt	Dyson

Virginia Slave Births Index, 1853-1865, Geographic Supplement

Sussex	Sussex	Sussex
Eason	Hardaway	Judkins
Edwards	Hargrave	King
Eldredge	Harris	Kitchen
Eldridge	Harrison	Ladd
Ellis	Harriss	Lamb
Eppes	Hartley	Land
Evans	Hartly	Lane
Faison	Harvell	Leavell
Fannin	Hatch	Lee
Feild	Hawthorne	Leonard
Field	Heath	Lessenburg
Fitzhugh	Hill	Levell
Foster	Hood	Lewis
Freeman	Horn	Lilly
Gay	Horne	Little
Gee	Howell	Magee
Gilliam	Howle	Malone
Gilliam (Est)	Hunnicut	Mangram
Graves	Hunnicutt	Mangrum
Green	Hunt	Mangum
Gregg	Hurst	Marable
Grigg	Inman	Mason
Grizzard	Ivey	Massenburg
Gwaltney	Jackson	Mathews
Haddon	Jarrad	Mayes
Hale	Jarratt	McGlanon
Hales	Jarrett	McGlaure
Hall	Jennings	McGlemore
Hammond	Johnson	McGlere
Hansberger	Jones	McLemore

Virginia Slave Births Index, 1853-1865, Geographic Supplement

Sussex	**Sussex**	**Sussex**
Moore	Remington	Turner
Morris	Richardson	Wade
Moyler	Riddick	Walton
Neblet	Rives	Ware
Neblett	Robinson	Watkins
Nelms	Rodgers	West
Niblett	Rogers	Westbrook
Nicholson	Rollings	Wharton
Northcross	Rose	White
Overton	Rowland	Whitehorn
Owen	Rowzee	Whitehorne
Pace	Saunders	Whitmore
Parham	Scott	Wilborne
Parker	Seaborn	Wilkerson
Parson	Seward	Williams
Parsons	Shands	Williamson
Pate	Simmons	Winfield
Peebles	Sledge	Wood
Pennington	Smith	Wrenn
Person	Southall	Wyar
Peters	Spain	Wyatt
Pettoway	Spires	Wynne
Pleasants	Stephenson	**Sussex/Dinwiddie**
Pond	Stewart	Crawford
Pope	Sykes	**Sussex/Petersburg**
Potts	Taylor	Bott
Presson	Thornton	Stephenson
Prince	Thorp	**Sussex/Southampton**
Raines	Tresson	Drewry
Reese	Tudor	Stephenson

Sussex/TX	Tazewell	Tazewell
Harrison	Estille	Louthen
Tazewell	Francisco	Lowder
Baldwin	Fudge	Lowthen
Barnes	George	Lyons
Barns	Gibson	Matney
Baylor	Gillespie	Mays
Beaham	Gillispie	Meek
Benham	Graham	Moore
Bishop	Green	Murphy
Boggs	Greever	Owens
Bogle	Gregory	Peery
Bowen	Hankins	Reynolds
Bowman	Harman	Saint Clair
Brown	Harmon	Sarver
Buchanan	Harriss	Shannon
Burts	Harrisson	Smith
Carpenter	Harthorn	Smyth
Cecil	Hawthorn	Spotts
Chapman	Hedrick	Sprinkle
Compton	Heninger	Steele
Cox	Higgenbotham	Stras
Crockett	Higginbotham	Suiter
Crump	Holmes	Suter
Custard	Honaker	Taylor
Davidson	Howard	Thompson
Davis	Johnston	Tiffany
Deskins	Jones	Ward
Dillard	Kindrick	Watkins
Dills	Layne	Watts
Estile	Litz	White

Virginia Slave Births Index, 1853-1865, Geographic Supplement

Tazewell	Warren	Warren
Witten	Davidson	Kendrick
Yost	Davison	Kenner
Young	Dodson	King
Tazewell/Russell	Dulaney	Laurence
Brown	Dulany	Lawrence
Warren	Earle	Leach
Allen	Earles	Leary
Armistead	Eastham	Lehew
Armstead	Ewan	Leith
Ash	Ewing	Lewin
Ashby	Finnell	Maddox
Barbee	Fish	Marshall
Beaty	Fristoe	Massie
Beech	Funkhouser	McDonald
Bennett	Gardner	McKay
Boone	Garrison	Melton
Bowen	Grant	Menefee
Bowman	Green	Menifee
Boyd	Hall	Millan
Brown	Hansbrough	Miller
Buck	Harrison	Milton
Carr	Haynie	Morehead
Carson	Heath	Murphy
Carter	Hite	Murray
Churchill	Hoard	Myers
Cline	Hopewell	Neville
Conrad	Hord	Oliver
Cook	Jacob	Overall
Criser	Jacobs	Petty
Cunningham	John	Powers

Warren	Warren	Warwick
Pulliam	Winsbrough	Milstead
Richards	Winsburrow	Patrick
Richardson	Woodrack	Seburn
Rickard	Woodward	Shield
Ridgeway	Wright	Smelt
Ridgway	**Warren/Fauquier**	Tabb
Robertson	Glasscock	Tucker
Robinson	Maddox	Wade
Roy	**Warrenton**	Whitaker
Rust	Jackson	Wilbern
Scroggin	**Warwick**	Wootten
Short	Brown	Wynne
Shrot	Corbin	Young
Sillman	Crafford	**Warwick/KY**
Simpson	Curtis	Marrow
Spengler	Fitchett	**Washington**
Stinson	Gambol	Alderson
Tait	Garrow	Appling
Taite	Green	Bailey
Templeman	Grubb	Baker
Thomas	Harwood	Beatie
Thompson	Haughton	Beattie
Timberlake	Haynes	Beaty
Triplett	Jones	Bondurant
Turner	Lee	Bradley
Updike	Lewelling	Brown
Vannort	Marrow	Buchanan
Vanvort	McCenney	Byars
Wheatley	McIntosh	Campbell
Williamson	McKenney	Carmack

Virginia Slave Births Index, 1853-1865, Geographic Supplement

Washington	Washington	Washington
Carpenter	Greenway	Meadley
Cawood	Hagy	Merchant
Clapp	Hamilton	Miller
Clark	Hanby	Milliard
Clarke	Hawthorn	Mock
Coleman	Hayter	Montgomery
Corry	Henderson	Moon
Crockett	Horne	Moore
Cummings	Hunter	Moorman
Cunningham	Hutton	Morison
Davenport	Johnston	Morrell
Davidson	Jones	Newland
Davis	Keller	Nuckols
Duff	Kelly	Orr
Dunn	Kesner	Parrott
Edmondson	King	Pemberton
Edwards	Lathim	Preston
Ellington	Lathin	Price
Fickle	Legard	Rambo
Fields	Litchfield	Reid
Fleenor	Logan	Rhea
Forest	Loyd	Roberts
Fulcher	Lynch	Robertson
Fullen	Maiden	Robinson
Galliher	Mallicote	Rodafer
Gardner	McCall	Roe
Gibson	McChesney	Rogers
Glenn	McConnell	Rosenbalm
Goodson	McCormack	Rush
Gray	McQuown	Sheffey

Virginia Slave Births Index, 1853-1865, Geographic Supplement

Washington	Westmoreland	Westmoreland
Shugart	Bailey	Fones
Skinner	Bailor	Forbes
Smith	Baker	Garnett
Smyth	Balderson	Gawen
Snapp	Barrack	George
Snodgrass	Baylor	Goldin
Spunier	Bayne	Goldman
Spurrier	Beale	Gouldin
Stewart	Bernard	Graham
Stickley	Blackwell	Griffith
Strother	Bowie	Gutridge
Susong	Bransom	Haley
Talbert	Branson	Hall
Tate	Brockenbrough	Hardwick
Teeter	Brown	Harvey
Teetor	Carter	Healey
Tool	Chandler	Henage
Trigg	Chowning	Hinage
Vance	Costin	Hudson
Wallace	Courtney	Hungerford
Whitaker	Crabb	Hunter
White	Craddock	Hutt
Willoughby	Critcher	Jackson
Wisely	Croxton	Jett
Woods	Deatley	Jones
Worley	Dishman	King
Washington/Campbell	Ditty	Kirk
Jennings	Dozier	Lampkin
Westmoreland	Edwards	Lawrence
Atwill	English	Lefever

Virginia Slave Births Index, 1853-1865, Geographic Supplement

Westmoreland	Westmoreland	Williamsburg
Lewis	Robinson	Bargiga
Locke	Rust	Barlow
Lyell	Sanford	Barzira
Marmaduke	Smoot	Blain
Martin	Spence	Bowden
Mayo	Spillman	Bowman
Monroe	Spilman	Bright
Monros	Stark	Charles
Montgomery	Stephen	Clabourn
Mothershead	Sutton	Claibourne
Munroe	Taliaferro	Coke
Murphy	Tallant	Cole
Nash	Taylor	Coleman
Newton	Thomas	Custis
Noel	Thrift	Dey
Northam	Tommas	Dix
Northern	Turner	Durfey
Omohundro	Tyler	Galt
Parker	Walker	Garett
Payne	Waring	Garrett
Peirce	Washington	Harrell
Polk	Watson	Heller
Pope	Weaver	Henley
Porter	Wheelwright	Hope
Powers	Wilkins	Jones
Pursel	Wilson	Joyner
Reed	Wright	Lipscomb
Rhodham	**Williamsburg**	Lively
Rice	Armistead	Lucas
Robb	Bailey	Mason

Virginia Slave Births Index, 1853-1865, Geographic Supplement

Williamsburg	**Winchester**	**Wise**
Maupin	Brown	Snodgrass
McCandlish	Burwell	**Wythe**
Minor	Campbell	Allison
Munford	Campbill	Boyd
Newman	Drew	Brown
Peachy	Fuller	Browning
Piggott	Glenn	Buchanan
Powell	Harrison	Buck
Richardson	Hartman	Caffee
Saunders	Jackson	Calfee
Savage	Kiger	Cassel
Smith	McCormick	Cassell
Sweeney	Miller	Cassle
Taylor	Morris	Catlett
Tucker	Newman	Chaffin
Vest	Parker	Chafin
Waller	Ridley	Chapman
Walter	Seevers	Cleaveland
Warren	Seiver	Corvin
Watkins	Smith	Crockett
Wilmer	Stephenson	Davis
Wynne	Tucker	Earhart
Williamsburg/York	Zircle	Ehart
Powell	**Wise**	Ewing
Winchester	Dickinson	Fisher
Anderson	Gilly	Floyd
Baines	Grey	Fulton
Boyd	Hoge	Ganaway
Brent	Lee	Gannaway
Brooking	Richmond	Gibboney

Virginia Slave Births Index, 1853-1865, Geographic Supplement

Wythe	Wythe	Wythe
Gleaves	Painter	Thomley
Gose	Pence	Tilson
Graham	Percival	Trigg
Grayson	Perkins	Umbarger
Groseclose	Pickle	Waddle
Grubb	Pierce	Waid
Haller	Piper	Ward
Hoge	Porter	Wisely
Holston	Raper	**Wythe/Pulaski**
Hounshell	Repass	Hoge
Hudson	Rich	**Wythe/Roanoke Co**
Hufford	Richardson	Lewis
Hurst	Roberson	**York**
Hurt	Rosenbaum	Adams
Jackson	Rosenbum	Anderson
Keesling	Sagers	Belvin
Kegley	Sanders	Bryan
Kent	Sayers	Bryant
Kyle	Scott	Carmines
Lawson	Sexton	Carter
Mathews	Shaffer	Chapman
Matthews	Shannon	Cook
McGavock	Simmerman	Cooke
McTear	Spence	Cox
Moore	Stakes	Crockett
Morris	Steptoe	Crofford
Morrison	Straw	Curtis
Neff	Stuart	Davis
Newberry	Tate	Davison
Nuckolls	Terry	Dawson

Virginia Slave Births Index, 1853-1865, Geographic Supplement

York

Doisin
Dorsin
Earnest
Evans
Fletcher
Freeman
Garrett
Gray
Heath
Henley
Hogg
Hopkins
Howard
Ironmonger
James
Kirby
Kirley
Lee
Lennis
Linsey
Mahone
Martin
McCandlish
Messick
Minson
Montgomery
Moreland
Nelson
Norvell
Nottingham

York

Nowell
Patrick
Pettitt
Phillips
Power
Presson
Pumphre
Pumphrey
Ray
Rollins
Russell
Saunders
Savage
Selby
Sheannan
Shearman
Sheild
Shell
Sherman
Shield
Skinner
Smith
Tailer
Tennice
Tennis
Throckmorton
Throgmorton
Topping
Trockmorton
Wade

York

Waller
Warler
Warren
Waymouth
Western
Weston
Wheler
Whitaker
Wilson
Wornom
Wrett
Wynne

York/Warwick

Curtis

www.ingramcontent.com/pod-product-compliance
Lightning Source LLC
Chambersburg PA
CBHW070909270326
41927CB00011B/2507